STRESS NINJA

®

THE MINDSET NEEDED TO IDENTIFY, CONTROL, REDUCE AND EVEN ERADICATE STRESS IS THE SAME ONE NEEDED FOR SELF DEFENCE. STRESS IS THE ENEMY. CONTROL THE ENEMY AND YOU'LL BE A STRESS NINJA TOO...

KARL ROLLISON

This first edition first published in 2018.

Edited by: Conor Corderoy.

Stress Ninja Logo is a Registered Trademark.

Cover image & design© Karl Rollison.

Text © Karl Rollison.

Logo Design: Karl Rollison.

Photos and Illustrations: Karl Rollison.

For more information regarding this publication and other products, please visit the Stress Ninja website:

www.stress-ninja.com

ISBN 978 1 9164109 0 9

DEDICATED...

To my amazing wife Suzanne.
Thank you for your endless support and guidance and for
being the best human being ever bestowed on this spinning
planet xxx.

THANK YOU...

To Anne Jirsch for your professional guidance and continuous help, support and friendship.
To my editor Conor Corderoy for your patience, professional help and advice.
To Chris Meaden and Mary Beth Hazeldine (slightly better coaches than me) for giving me a push.

AND...

Thank you to my embarrassing second dad, lifelong friend and martial arts instructor
Sensei Norman Smithers (Dai Shihan).

My Martial Arts training partners and fantastic friends
Paul Oldland, Darren Cherry, Shawn Nagle and Phil 'Wendy' White.
Thanks for being gentle with me over the years.

ALSO...

To my lovely mates Lee Velleman, Carl Jenkinson, Dave Willats, John Davies, Mark Bunyan, Andre Rayson, Big Rich Strang, Nathan Parry, Adam Kennard, Steve Howes, Chris Neville and Matt Gillmore for telling me to stop crying, man up and keep going...and when all else fails, to Sean Hackett for the occasional slap when I need one.

A Special thank you to my cat 'Alien' for sitting on my shoulders and keeping my neck warm throughout the whole writing process.

CONTENTS

INTRODUCTION

The glass of red wine slipped from my hand and smashed onto the floor, seconds later I slid down the wall to join it. I started sobbing uncontrollably. I'd rarely cried before but now I couldn't stop. I placed my head in my hands and rocked back and forth. I was vaguely aware of a stabbing sensation in my forehead. Did a full mental breakdown physically hurt? Was it painful when one's sanity finally squeezed its way free? I looked at my hands and saw, with relief, a shard of glass protruding from deep in my left palm.

The wind lashed freezing rain against the window and roused me from my sobbing trance. It was the middle of January and the sky was almost as black as my mood. I slowly became aware of my surroundings. The only sound in the room was the high pitched whir of the laptop. The computer was also the only source of light, casting a blue white glow onto the wall from its empty Word document.

The report was now 2 weeks late and was due in the next morning 'without fail.' The document itself wasn't the problem. The fact that I was so stressed, exhausted and anxious that I couldn't actually focus on anything was. I worked at the flagship office of the biggest bank in the world in the centre of London. When I got home in the evenings I would change clothes, and then drive to my other office to work on my business. I was literally killing myself with work. I didn't just have a creative block about this particular document, but about every aspect of my life. I had a beautiful house, three cars, seven bespoke suits, a collection of expensive watches, lots of money, lots of friends, no debt - and I was miserable.

I looked over at the laptop, it reminded me of a trapdoor, a portal to another world. If it had lead to a place where I just ceased to exist I would have passed through it in a heartbeat.

The feeling terrified me. To try and bring myself back to some kind of normality I switched on the TV. The room was filled instantly with the light and vibrancy of a travel programme about the remote islands of Fiji. I gazed at the beautiful white sand, turquoise waters and paradisal settings and felt a yearning in my heart, but Fiji may as well have been a different planet. I rose and looked at myself in the mirror. I was wearing a mask of tears, wine and blood. I looked and felt small, vulnerable and pathetic.

What happened next still makes the hairs on the back of my neck stand up. I had a realisation, like I'd just solved a lifelong problem. I started laughing. Could it be that easy? I had a tangible feeling of pins and needles, and warmth, flowing from my head to my toes. Whenever I think about that wonderful light, energy-charged feeling there is only one word that comes to mind, and it's a beautiful word I have never used in a conversation or sentence before or since. That word is 'BLISS.'

I felt like I suddenly knew the meaning of life and, in a way, I did. I marched into the kitchen, removed the glass from my hand and washed my face, the whole time chuckling to myself. But this was not the laughter of a madman - quite the opposite. I bandaged my hand and went purposefully back into the lounge. I stopped at the mirror on my way and checked my reflection, I seemed to be glowing. I looked strong. I was back. I smiled at myself and looked over at the laptop. For the first time in months it wasn't an object of terror. It still resembled a trapdoor, but rather than a portal of doom it was now a doorway to paradise, and I knew how to get there. I sat down at the computer with the level of excitement usually reserved for small children at Christmas. I started typing. I wrote all night.

Even though I hadn't slept all night I felt supercharged, I felt like I could breathe properly again. I kept giggling. Usually I wanted the train to go as slow as possible so I could use the precious time to relax, but not this morning. This morning I sat forward with excitement.

At the office, I thrust the document into Mike's hand before he'd had the chance to take his coat off.

'It's not the document you were expecting I'm afraid.'

Mike scanned the paper, then looked at me, confused, and said 'Resignation letter? I don't understand. What are you doing? You have an amazing career here!'

'Give it to someone else. I don't want it anymore.'

'Look, if you want more money let's talk about it. Are you going to another bank?'

Mike was a big Danish guy and the best boss I'd ever had. I threw my arms around him and gave him a big hug and kissed him on the cheek. He was trying not to laugh and was shaking his head in a "crazy Englishman" type of way I've seen many times in my life.

I said, 'No Mike.' My voice cracking with emotion, 'I'm going to Fiji!'

I wrote two documents that night, the resignation letter took 20 minutes, the other one took 5 hours, it was a comprehensive bucket list that contained hundreds of detailed items including attending the Silverstone school of motor racing, gaining my competition licence and racing Formula Fords, SCUBA diving the great barrier reef, doing the highest bungee jump in the world, swimming with dolphins, driving across New Zealand, climbing a glacier, eating noodles overlooking Hong Kong harbour, drinking a Singapore sling at Raffles, touring around Australia, Thailand, America and of course, hopping around the islands of Fiji.

I spent the next two years ticking them off, I'm now on my 4th bucket list.

So why am I telling you this? Because the chances are, if you are reading this book, you are experiencing prolonged stress. Stress is pressure. If pressure is applied to anything for long enough things happen, it can only be resisted for a certain period of time. As humans we can snap. This can mean physically, emotionally or mentally, and not one of them is good. So we have two options, resist the pressure or release the pressure. One is a short term fix and the other a more permanent measure. This book will help you identify which one you are experiencing and give you the knowledge and techniques to successfully deal with them.

SO WHY STRESS NINJA? Because Ninjas aren't the strongest, fastest or toughest fighters, but they are amongst the smartest. The concept of Ninjutsu is to understand your enemy. Knowledge can overcome ANY enemy. Knowledge is Power. As you will see in the next few chapters stress is the NUMBER ONE enemy of mankind. It was knowledge that came to my aid that cold January evening, I suddenly understood that I'd got myself into the situation and relinquished myself to the enemy and that, if I'd given control over to stress then I could just as easily take it back again.

So how do I know so much about stress? Well, for a start I'm a massive stress head and everything I've done since that winter's night has been to understand stress. I am a registered Harley Street Hypnotherapist who specialises in corporate stress management... Oh yeah, I've also studied and taught Ninjutsu all over the world for nearly 30 years. That's the other cool thing about this book, it's also a self defence manual! If you pay attention and practice the techniques, you'll be a Stress Ninja too.

You will notice two main symbols that run throughout this book:

The represents the ancient scrolls (or Makimomo). These were used in the 1000 year old martial art of Ninjutsu to transfer knowledge and skills from master to student. I'm using this icon to highlight a particularly important piece of **information** I want you to take on board. I have called this *a scroll of enlightenment.*

The equates to the weapon that was used in Ninjutsu, the throwing star (or Shuriken). In this instance I'm using this icon to represent a particularly powerful **technique** I would like to draw your attention to. Unlike the scroll, this actually requires your participation. I am calling this *the star of empowerment.*

This book can be used as a reference guide where you can flick through and look for the above symbols. Doing this will help you in every aspect of your life. However, if you want a completely different and far more rewarding experience, please go through it in the logical order, chapter by chapter, and practise every technique before you move on to the next. It will change your life. I'm not saying this lightly. Just the planning alone of this book has taken me years. It is an expansion, a more detailed version, of what I do with my clients, and I've helped many people over the years.

Stress Ninja says...

"You should be proud of yourself for deciding to master stress rather than allowing it to master you."

01. KNOWLEDGE IS POWER

Do you have a favourite quote? A sentence that perhaps spoke to you personally as soon as you read it? A short statement that somehow gives you strength and inspiration? Maybe you were so motivated by these words that you decided to have them permanently etched on your body?

The thing I love about quotes, idioms and clichés is that some might be thousands of years old yet they are as relevant today as they were then. It also makes me laugh when someone uses one of these thought provoking pearls of wisdom, passed up from our ancestors as advice, in the right context and with good intentions, and then gets accused of being unoriginal.

The reason some of them are still used is because they are still valid. My favourite quote is

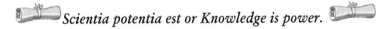**Scientia potentia est or Knowledge is power.**

You could interpret this in different ways, but for me it means that to understand something is empowerment. Empowerment is confidence, therefore to know something eliminates the fear of it. When you start something new, whether it's a sport, a college course, a new business or job, you will experience fear. You have to. We are programmed to fear the unknown. This keeps us alive and safe and has done so for millions of years.

The more proficient, confident and knowledgeable you become, the less fear you feel. This is the same with anything in life, the more you understand how something works, the less scary it is. Take Stress, the more you understand what it is - how it works, why it's there, how we respond to it, how to identify it and most important, how to deal with it - the less of a problem it is.

When I see corporate clients in their office who are experiencing work related stress, I usually start off by doing a quick, detailed presentation on exactly what stress is. What tends to happen is they sit there with furrowed brows nodding politely, wondering why this is relevant (probably like you are now). Then I see a shift, a change in their demeanour, energy, expression or physical position. They may lean back on their chair and say something like 'Oh, that explains it', or something of the sort, that tells me they have started to understand. Then I know I've got them, it's like I've found their valve and I've started to turn it to release the pressure. 'What, relieving stress just by explaining how it works?' I hear you say. Yes! *Scientia potentia est.*

EVERYONE IS JUST AS SCARED AS YOU!

When it comes to the stress response, no one escapes its clutches, NO ONE! Forget the sharp end of stress, *e.g.* moving home or financial problems. Just living day to day is becoming ever more stressful.

I believe this is compounded by Social Media because people only ever share their strengths and achievements, usually accompanied by shiny triumphant images, and very rarely their failures and weaknesses. But that is not reality.

We all know our lives aren't perfect, yet we compare our 'behind the scenes' existence with other peoples broadcast 'highlights.' We've all probably seen someone posting a picture of themselves with the caption 'just woke up' when in reality they've just spent an hour doing their hair and makeup and taken 100 photos until they got the right one. We are daily and repeatedly fed the message that everyone else copes better than we do, but in reality, in real life, if we see someone dealing with a stressful situation calmly and efficiently, then there are a few things that could be going on:

1. They are so attuned to dealing with that situation in that context that they are now completely desensitised to it, a seasoned pro. They have seen and experienced every connotation of the event and its outcome. To put it another way, they are in their *COMFORT ZONE*. In this scenario just because WE would be stressed, it doesn't mean they are.

2. They APPEAR to be the pinnacle of calm and control, the definition of cool. However, they may just be great at *HIDING* how they really feel.

3. They APPEAR to be the pinnacle of calm and control, the definition of cool. However, they may just be great at *CONTROLLING* how they really feel.

Let's have a quick look at examples:

1.   **Comfort Zone**. Maybe we would be stressed cooking Christmas dinner for loads of friends and family, but I bet we wouldn't be if we were professional chefs.

2.   **Hiding**. We may think that ignoring our feelings and emotions means they'll disappear, but we are just building pressure. When pressure gets too high, things happen. I used to work with a Trader in the City. He was the manifestation of cool, calm and collected. Nothing fazed him. We all admired him for never getting stressed. However, he did get stressed. He just never admitted to it. He committed suicide.

3.   **Controlling**. This is what this book is about. To do this we have to be honest and brave. Honest enough to admit to ourselves that we feel fear and anxiety. Then brave enough to seek out solutions, and brave enough to keep going despite wanting to run away.

Remember: anyone can appear in control if they are in their comfort zone. But most people, most of the time, appear cool on the outside when in fact they are just as scared as we are underneath.

> **Be like a duck, my mother used to tell me. Remain calm on the surface and paddle like hell underneath. -Michael Caine (well, his mum actually).**

THE POWER OF EMPOWERMENT

All humans react in pretty much the same way when facing a negative situation. This next section is one of the most empowering pieces of knowledge that I can pass on. (One of the scrolls of enlightenment

( ) I mentioned - there are many others in this book).

I've been successfully teaching Women self defence and awareness for many years and I absolutely love it. Women tend to be so much more honest than men about fears and anxiety and I always learn loads.

> *If men could drop the macho shields and just admit that we are all just scared little boys the World would be a far better place. —Karl Rollison*

I was recently speaking to a new group on one of my courses. One of the women told us of a recent incident when she was out jogging by herself in her local park. There was no one else around and this guy stepped out from behind a bush. He was waving his arms to stop her. He was agitated, dirty and emotional. She initially feared the worst. As it transpired this poor guy had lost his beloved dog and he was asking her if she'd seen it on her travels. 'That's why I'm here,' she said, 'I was shocked at my reaction. I felt weak and my legs just seemed to turn to jelly. If he had been an attacker I would have been at his mercy.'

I've heard this so many times before, this was my response:

'Actually, your legs never turned to jelly and you hadn't suddenly become weakened by the encounter. In fact, the exact opposite had happened. What you were experiencing was actually a massive surge in oxygen rich, adrenaline saturated blood flooding your arms and legs to enable you to attack or run...or both. In many cases this natural reaction is so extreme that you can become faster and stronger than your assailant, even if they are bigger than you. After all, their body will be in a high state of arousal, but never as high as yours.'

A Zen master was out for a walk with one of his students when they noticed a fox chasing a rabbit.

"According to an ancient saying the rabbit will escape," said the master.

"Not so," replied the student, "the fox is faster."

"Nevertheless, the rabbit will elude the fox," the master stated.

"How can you be so certain?" asked the student.

"The fox is running for its' dinner. The rabbit is running for its' life."

-----Anonymous

I have known this piece of information to generate big changes in people's confidence and self-awareness. Hopefully it will with you too. Our stress response is just another tool. We just need to learn how to use it.

Most things can be explained. When it comes to stress, understanding it reduces its negative effects.

Someone asked me recently if we could totally eliminate stress. Well, probably with the right drugs or surgery, but it's there to protect us and has been doing a fantastic job for a few million years, after all:

" If stress had never existed then neither would we". – Karl Rollison

When we talk about stress, it is important to understand that we are actually talking about a physiological process that is happening in our bodies. We have a system called the Autonomic Nervous System (ANS). This is completely automatic and outside of our awareness. The ANS controls things like our heart rate, breathing, urination, digestion etc. This system is divided into two further subsystems: the Sympathetic and Parasympathetic Nervous Systems. When we encounter danger, the Hypothalamus in our brain mobilises an army of natural chemicals and floods our bodies with Cortisol and Adrenaline. This is our Sympathetic Nervous System taking over. If we think of the ANS as a Sea Saw then our system has flipped to one side. Everything in life and the universe is about balance and we can balance our ANS by powering up our Parasympathetic Nervous System. Don't worry, it's not too complicated, it can't be; I understand it. However, knowledge is

21

power and to understand how this works is SO important. I will explore all of this in more detail in the next chapter and I've included real world examples for clarity.

Stress Ninja says...

"Knowledge really IS power and YOU are the one that has decided to seek this knowledge. This will lead to empowerment...YOUR empowerment to be precise."

02.   RUN OR RUMBLE

This is a process that keeps us safe and has done for millions of years. It's used in one form or another by every creature on the planet. You may be using it right now. This particular name for the process is one I made up years ago for my self defence classes. You probably know it as...

THE FIGHT OR FLIGHT RESPONSE.

If we were to put live human cells in a Petri dish and put nutrients on one side of the dish and toxins on the other, what would happen? I'll tell you, the cells would move towards the food and away from the danger.

So basically we are dealing with two states, moving **forwards** or moving **backwards**. Moving backwards is **protection,** and equates to our **flight or fight instinct,** whereas moving forwards is **growth**. The thing is, we can't do both at the same time.

As humans we only have a certain amount of blood in our bodies and when we are in protection this supply is redirected away from non-essential systems into the areas that will enable us to stay alive in the face of danger. Our immune and digestive systems are very blood intensive and are switched off. What's really scary is that our higher brain functions are also part of the budget cuts – we actually become less intelligent. That might not sound like a very good system but don't forget this was developed when we were cavemen. I'm going to explore this in more detail later but for now I have included some scenarios to explain all of this in real terms.

Fight or flight - acute stress: (Scenario 1)

John is walking to his car after a hard day at work. It's late at night, the car park is dark and he is so preoccupied with his thoughts that he doesn't notice the three guys following him. Suddenly he is surrounded. The guy in front of him pulls a knife and demands his wallet. John tries to run but he has no exit. He hands over his phone, wallet and watch and, thankfully, they disappear into the night. John is unharmed.

Externally John was unharmed and if he contextualised it properly (there was nothing he could do, he got away unhurt and he only lost stuff that can be replaced) he should get along without having long term affects. But what happened to John internally? Let's have a look. When John realised he was in danger:

- The Hypothalamus in his brain teamed up with his pituitary and adrenal glands to produce massive amounts of Adrenalin and Cortisol.

- He started breathing in longer, harder and faster than he breathed out in order to load up his blood with Oxygen.

- The blood that usually feeds his immune system was diverted to his arms and legs to allow him to stand and fight or run away (fight or flight).

- His digestive system was switched off so that the massive amount of blood used for this system could also be diverted to his extremities to allow him to run or fight.

- With his digestive system halted the stomach needed to purge, this is why people vomit (or worse) in moments of fear and stress. Purging also makes us physically lighter allowing us to be faster and more agile.

- He felt strange sensations in his legs as they were loaded with adrenaline.

- His mouth went dry, it will not be needed (when this system was first developed it was usually to deal with wild animals...they are not great conversationalists).

- His heart felt like it was going to explode as its rate and blood pressure increase dramatically to deliver oxygen rich blood around his system.

- His eyes dilated to allow as much detail into his brain as possible.

- Time seemed to distort as he started to process massive amounts of data.

- His higher brain functions stopped - intellectualising the situation will slow down reactions and increase the danger.

This is a horrible situation but believe it or not his Sympathetic nervous system has worked perfectly, exactly the way it was designed to, millions of years ago. The thing is, back then, we only needed this system when we were confronted with a hungry sabre tooth tiger and, to use a software analogy that was version 1.0. The problem is we are still on the same version, and it can't differentiate between a threat to our life (acute stress) and every day pressures (chronic stress).

> *Our environment has developed constantly over the last million years and is now on about version 1809246.09 (release 2) yet our mechanisms to cope with it are still on version 1.0 (beta). – Karl Rollison*

This leads us on nicely to what this book is mainly about, the cause of most of the problems in the world today, the reason we now have colloquialisms like 'trolley rage' and probably the reason you are reading this book in the first place. We are all suffering from varying degrees of...chronic stress.

Fight or flight – chronic stress: (scenario 2)

Imagine this scene (this is a concoction of various people I've helped over the years):

Peter wakes up every morning before his alarm goes off. He has worked at the same company for many years. He despises his job but is hanging out for the remote possibility of a large redundancy payout. He is paranoid that the company will try to sack him before they have to pay him out, therefore he works harder than he should. After all, he has a large mortgage, bills, car payments etc. He is the first person at work in the morning. He doesn't sleep well and is on constant alert throughout the night in case he receives an email that may need his immediate attention. He doesn't want this to disturb his wife so he sleeps in the spare room. He usually stays awake worrying about losing his job, house, wife and ending up on the streets. He frequently takes a sleeping tablet. He works on his laptop on the train on his way to and from work. He takes and makes calls and sends and receives emails in front of the television, at breakfast, at dinner even when out with his wife, friends and family. Consequently he no longer gets invited out. He is overweight and very unfit but has no time for exercise. He is always tired so he consumes massive amounts of coffee, energy drinks, diet soda, and sweets, and for extra comfort, chocolate. He also eats fast food and processed food for convenience. He can't seem to focus on his work and whenever he gets called into his a meeting or has to do a presentation his mind goes blank. This has caused him panic attacks. Part of his job is innovation but he hasn't had an original idea in months, adding to his woes. His overall health is poor; he has constant headaches, stomach aches, colds, flu, indigestion, fatigue, anxiety and chest pains. To wind down after work, and to help him sleep, he has started drinking heavily and smoking. He never has a solid quality sleep and he is usually awake before the alarm goes off.

So let's look at what's happening here.

Peter is in a toxic environment, but rather than leave he has created a belief framework in his head that is not necessarily based on fact. He has no proof that his company is trying to oust him, but he has created a whole chain of negative effects in his mind that will occur 'when' they sack him. Basically, he is in a state of burnout, this happens when we feel OVERWHELMED and out of CONTROL. Also:

- He feels he needs to respond to emails. He is not expected to, but by doing so he has set a precedent for his own availability, therefore he receives more emails in the middle of the night. This has put huge strain on his marriage. This affects his sleep.

- He has actually contaminated his social life and relaxation time with work. He no longer gets invited out because when he does, he just stares at his phone.

- He has infected his home with work. He responds to emails and calls in every room in his house therefore he has contaminated his home with the office. As a result he has no safe haven - no down time so no safe zone. He has no sanctuary therefore he is CONSTANTLY at work.

- The protective stress hormone Cortisol is at a constantly elevated rate. This will negatively affect the production of Melatonin which is vital for sleep.

- With the lack of sleep and sleeping tablets he is constantly tired. To compensate for this he consumes large quantities of caffeine. This is a toxic substance.

- To wind down he is consuming alcohol and nicotine. These are toxic.

- He eats convenience foods, these are full of preservatives, salts, sugars and trans-fatty acids. The body can't process these and treats them as toxins.

- He makes feeble attempts at being healthy by drinking diet drinks. Most artificial sweeteners are absolute poisons and our body sees them as such. It has also been proven that these generate massive hunger and cause us to eat more. (More about this later).

- He also intakes large amounts of sugar. Sugar is not dangerous per se but large quantities are. The brain is constantly stressed trying to work out how much insulin to produce, its primary job is to protect us. It stresses if it thinks it is failing, triggering a stress cycle.

- The above toxins are being consumed into a faulty system. With varying levels of perceived external stress his digestive system is operating at varying degrees of efficiency.

- With the constant flux of fight or flight his immune system is massively suppressed, sometimes switching off all together, this is why he is always ill, snowballing the worry of being sacked.

- He can't seem to focus and his mind goes blank. When our stress response gets too high our higher brain functions are switched off. This is a natural situation but Pete thinks he just can't cope, causing him worry that he is seen as incompetent.

• He is full of self doubt. This is exaggerated by the constant din of Peter's internal dialogue, that little voice that we all carry around in our heads.

• He has a lack of energy, therefore a lack of motivation.

• Peter THINKS he is being attacked externally and is causing an INTERNAL attack, therefore he is in Protection mode. He has switched off his growth mechanism. He has switched off his creativity and destroyed his innovation.

In scenario 1 above there is no ambiguity and there are no assumptions, John was under attack. However, the irony of scenario 2 is that Peter may actually be highly valued as a staff member. It is also possible he is not expected to be on constant call for his company. But none of this matters because it's Peter's *PERCEPTION* of his environment that is causing him all these problems. All of them are self inflicted, and I see this happening all the time. He is making himself ill just with his thought processes. Worse than this, he is actually killing himself. Don't believe me? You've heard of the placebo effect right? Well, have you heard of the nocebo effect? Well, both are very valid, very real and EXTREMELY powerful. The placebo effect can cure people with false medication. This generates a BELIEF that this will aid them in their recovery. The nocebo effect can cause harm by generating the opposite belief. These effects are VERY real and have been independently, clinically tested and verified throughout the world. We'll talk about these a bit later.

So, our perception of our environment is everything. **Reality never matters as much as the reality we have created inside our own heads.**

We choose how we see things and we choose how we respond to what we see. And once we decide to take responsibility for our perception and our responses, we can then decide to change them. We can, effectively, override our software with a bit of knowledge.

Knowledge is power.

If you'd like to explore these concepts in greater detail search for Bruce Lipton PhD online and check out one of his lectures, particularly the fascinating 'Biology of Belief'.

Stress Ninja says...

"In my experience, if you've read this far then you probably already know more about stress than pretty much anyone else around you."

03.   HOW STRESS KILLS

This is so important that I decided to devote a whole chapter to it.

Everyone knows that stress is bad for our health, and I will be covering the different effects that it has on us throughout this book, but first I want to shake you up a bit. I need you to take this seriously because if you are stressed you will eventually meet...

THE OPPORTUNISTIC BADDIES

Read this statement:

'They are the opportunistic baddies. They lie there waiting in the shadows. They are waiting for the right time to attack you. They know you, they know you well. And they are waiting for the right time to strike! To cause you damage. To hurt you...to kill you!'

Which of the scenarios from the previous Chapter does this statement best apply to? Number 1 or number 2? You think I'm talking about the first one? I'm referring to nasty criminals who are looking for an appropriate victim? Well, it could be, but I'm actually talking about number 2! I'm talking about opportunist micro-organisms.

> '*Opportunistic micro-organisms* are *typically non-pathogenic* **micro-organisms** *that act as a pathogen in certain circumstances. They lie dormant for long periods of time until the host's immune system is suppressed, and then they take that opportunity to attack.*'

So there you are. We have gone through a bacteria, pollution filled world and been hoovering up toxins and loading our systems with dormant pathogens. When your immune system hits a low, Bingo! Do you see now the absolute importance of reducing stress? By finding a way to unwind? Still not convinced?

Stress hormones are so good at turning off our immune system that they are actually administered to people who have received new organs, to prevent rejection!

So, clearly, all stress is bad for us, right? Nope! All will be revealed as you go through this book. Our job is not to avoid stress altogether, but to understand and manage it. The right amount of stress keeps us motivated to move forward. When we are moving forward we are growing. When we are growing we are happy. We just need to find our own personal sweet spot of stress. Everything has a sweet spot. If we drive our car in 3rd gear and the revs are too low the car will rumble and grumble, we'll still be moving but it's not a nice experience and it's no good for the car. If we drive too fast in that gear the engine will be screaming in protest. Again, it isn't a nice experience and it's bad for the car.

We can feel when a car is delivering smooth, strong acceleration. When the engine is operating at its optimum speed, this is called the 'power band' or 'sweet spot.' There is even an optimum band within this range, this is where the power output and the fuel efficiency are at their combined peak.

Our job is to find our own *sweet,* sweet spot. This book will allow us to do just that. There are some important concepts, ideas and messages throughout this book - totally ridding ourselves of stress isn't one of them, but the concept of equilibrium and balance is. Remember this:

Everything in the Universe has a natural balance, even our relationship with the essence of life - drinking water. Not enough will kill us but did you know that slightly too much will kill us a whole lot quicker? -Karl Rollison

OK, LETS RECAP:

- To understand something removes the fear of it - very important with a killer like stress.

-We tend to compare our lives with everyone else's, this is a scourge of Social Media. In reality everyone is just as scared and insecure as we are!

-Sometimes just understanding a small, natural reaction to a stressful situation can generate massive empowerment.

  -There are two main states in life: Moving backwards or moving forwards. Moving backwards is for protection. Moving forward is for growth. We can only do one or the other never both at the same time.

04.   TAKE A BREAK

OK, let's take a break from the doom and gloom of stress because, although knowledge is power sometimes too much knowledge too fast can be overwhelming. Just like anything in life, theory is one thing but there is no substitute for experience, in this instance, experience means physical techniques. There are many techniques in this book that I have collected from around the world. I have tried, tested and modified them and they work. Some are quite involved, others are simpler. I want to start with a simple one.

I see techniques as gifts. I like to give my clients gifts. The great thing about this is that even if they don't use them, just the knowledge that they have them is in itself hugely empowering!

Remember the symbol represents a technique – a star of empowerment.

 The first technique. Something to get your teeth into.

Right, this is a very simple technique that anyone can do. In fact, we do it all the time and you've probably already done it today. Everyone does it and has been doing it since the beginning of time. It's something, as the title suggests, you can really get your teeth into. Still not sure? Well, it's chewing. Sounds too simple? Everything I do is simple. Knowledge is power and we can now employ this as a Stress Ninja tool.

I want you to use chewing when you need a boost. If you are feeling low, or you are about to step out of your comfort zone, or you are feeling overwhelmed. The great thing is that I don't have to show you HOW to chew - in this technique the power comes from explaining WHY it's so powerful. Millions of years ago we had basically two states of existence, resting or searching for food. When we were hunting or foraging for food we were out in the open, exposing ourselves to danger. When we were resting we were usually with our group, feeling safe and secure. The ultimate expression of this was eating. We would only eat when we felt safe. So, from a hardwired neurological perspective, we associate chewing with relaxing. When we chew our Oxytocin levels rise and our Cortisol levels fall. A lot of people use this mechanism subconsciously. It's called comfort eating. You can't sit around all day eating cakes and sweets. As you'll see later that generates massive stress in itself. No, you need to chew on good quality gum. I usually give out 'Rescue Remedy' chewing gum to my clients. You can buy this in most high street chemists. DO NOT eat gum with sugar or bad sweeteners, you want natural sweeteners. I'll explain this in later chapters.

OK, now, as I said we don't need to practise the art of chewing, but now we know we can use it as a tool whenever we need it. However, the next one is a little bit more involved. It is only breathing, but it's using breathing as a weapon against stress, rather than an automatic process for sustaining life.

 ### The 5/12 breathing technique

You can do this technique pretty much anywhere and, like any other technique, the more you do it the better you'll get.

Make a quick note of how stressed you feel right now from 0 to 10. (0 is not at all and 10 is extreme).

Wet the back of each had and blow on them. Keep that feeling clear in your mind.

Sit in a quiet place where you can fully relax. Sit with your back straight.

Close your eyes and place your hands on either side of your stomach just under your ribs.

Keeping your eyes closed gently look up as though looking at the inside of your eyebrows.

Breathe in through your mouth and at the same time imagine that you are breathing in through the back of your hands. This invites the abdomen and diaphragm to the party.

Breathe in deep and fill the lungs from top to bottom. Breathe in for the count of 5.

Pay attention to the pause between breaths.

Purse your lips and imagine you are trying to blow out a candle over the other side of the room. Breathe out of your mouth for the count of 12 or until your lungs are completely empty. If you do this right you will be aware of your stomach sucking in.

Repeat this as many times as you can but stop if you get dizzy.

Now, I want you to gauge your stress levels again from 0 to 10.

If you have done this properly this level will be considerably lower! When you breathe out longer than you breathe in you are powering up your parasympathetic nervous system. You are tipping your autonomic nervous system away from 'fight or flight' towards 'Rest & Digest.' I will delve deeper into this later on.

By the way, breathing with the stomach and really using the diaphragm might feel a bit odd at first, but guess what? That's how we ALL breathed when we were babies, we just forgot how to do it as we grew older. It amazes me to what extent everything involves breathing. It is the key to life and, as you'll see throughout this book, it is an amazing and powerful tool. Yet most people go through their lives only thinking about breathing when they experience difficulties with it.

So these are two useful techniques that will help us to defend ourselves against stress, because managing stress is self defence. It is absolutely *self defence.* If we are aware of how we respond to a situation we can control that response. We are then controlling ourselves. Self control is the essence of both martial arts **AND** stress management. How can we control our enemy if we can't control ourselves? All this talk of martial arts may lead us to think we would understand all of this a lot better if we had martial arts training? Well, that's nonsense. I want to share another really cool fact that most people who train hate:

Worldwide, more people with zero training have defended themselves successfully against violent attack, than highly trained martial artists have.

Now, in the next chapter I want to expand on this, and I've got a couple of extremely important questions to put to you...

Stress Ninja says...

"You should now start to see that it's YOU who is in the driving seat when it comes to stress. You're doing a great job. Keep going!"

05.   IMPORTANT QUESTIONS

I was initially going to put this section at the end of the book, but it's really important and I want you to start thinking about this as soon as possible. It will take a bit of bravery to read this section and answer the question, but I know you're serious about being a Stress Ninja, so I think you're ready!

I knew her socially and had heard that her partner had died. Her mother was really worried about her and asked me to have a word. She was doing two jobs, when she wasn't working she was looking after her kids. She was a great, strict mum. Her kids were fit, healthy, polite and well adjusted. The problem was that after they had eaten a healthy meal, had their allocated TV or game time (after finishing homework) and gone to bed, out came the cigarettes, alcohol, junk food, sweets and chocolate. She looked 15 years older than she was and, although her children were immaculate, she wore ill fitting clothes, had greasy hair, bad skin and was about 4 stone overweight and gaining.

'Who's the most important person in your life?'

'*My kids.*' *Was her immediate answer*

'*No, listen to the question*', *I asked again,* '*Who is THE most important PERSON in your life?*'

'*My Kids!*' *She'd obviously just chosen to hear the words* "*important*" *and*" *life*". *I went with it.*

'*OK, so you're stranded on a desert island with your two kids and you managed to make an emergency phone call before your phone died. You will be rescued in a week but you have enough food and water for a few days. It will mean extreme rationing, all three of you will be in a bad way when you get rescued but you'll be alive. What would you do?*'

'*I'd give my rations to my kids.*'

'*But you could die.*'

'*I don't care. I'm not going to watch my kids suffer.*'

'*But it would only be for a few days. Then you'd have the rest of your lives together. In fact you'd be closer because of it.*'

'*But I would still give them my food and water.*'

'*So, the kids would watch you die. If they somehow managed to survive without you, they would not have you to protect them going forward. They might even go into care. They would probably grow up with some eating disorder and suffer guilt for the rest of their lives, believing that they'd had a hand in your death. It's the same as when the oxygen masks drop down in an emergency on an aeroplane. The reason adults are told to attend to their own masks first is so they are clear headed enough to put the children's on afterwards. That way everyone lives and the kids don't have to wake up sweating in the middle of the night for the rest of their lives replaying the time mummy convulsed, went blind, dribbled and babbled incoherently before dying next to them on a plane.'*

I leant forward. 'NOW, you obviously love your kids and no one is disputing that, but without being a victim or a martyr...WHO is the most important person in your life?'

'I've never really thought about it like that...what would happen to them if I wasn't around anymore?' She thought for a while, looking off into the distance with an intent expression on her face, then said (her voice catching with emotion), 'My god, you're right, what WOULD happen to them if I died? I'm being selfish aren't I? I need to start looking after myself!'

So, I know you would probably die for your wife, husband, son, daughter, girlfriend, boyfriend, dad, mum, sister, hamster etc, and that's great and noble. But that's called love and guess what? You can't love someone from the grave. You can't care for someone from your coffin.

You can't share memories with someone when you're just a memory yourself! - Karl Rollison

So, accept it. I want you to take a few moments to think about all of the people that would be devastated if you died. Visualise your own funeral like a scene from a movie. See all of the people you know, crying and distraught. See people so destroyed by your death that they can't physically stand up, and need to be supported by others.

So the question stands by the gentleman concerned:

Question 1: WHO is THE most important person in YOUR life?

If you are serious about being a Stress Ninja your answer needs to be (and I want you to say this out loud).

I am THE most important person in MY life!

Now we get to the really important part.

Think, in detail about:

A person that drains you

A situation that makes you anxious

An environment that gives you chest pains

46

An intimidating work colleague or boss

In fact, think of anything, ANYTHING that makes you feel a negative emotion. Remember, there are two states: protection (moving backwards) or growth (moving forward). If a person, a thing, an environment or anything else makes you feel negative you are moving backwards. When you are in protection you are encouraging your opportunistic pathogens as in *Chapter 3.*

Whatever or whoever is causing us stress, that thing is reducing our time on this planet...Reducing the time we get to spend with the people we love and who love us. Don't underestimate this!

So are you going to read this book, find some of it interesting then forget about it or are you going to take this seriously? Because this isn't a game and you only have one life.

As I say to anyone who comes to my self defence classes due to bullying, or a corporate client who is suffering constant stress related chest pains at work, 'I've given you the information. Now WHAT are you going to do with it?!'

As I said previously, more untrained people successfully defend themselves against street attacks than do highly trained, seasoned martial artists.

The problem is that physical attacks are pretty obvious but everyday stresses can be more subtle and go unnoticed. This book will allow us to identify these negatives. However, once we know the enemy, the same attitude will be needed for us to deal with it. This attitude is indignation or 'I refuse to allow this to have control over me!'

Hopefully now we can understand the logline on the front of this book,

'The mindset needed to identify, control, reduce and even eradicate stress is the same one needed for self defence.'

Before we move on I want to put it another way:

Every possible form of stress is out there waiting for us. This book will help us identify them. It will help us monitor the way we cope with them. It will give us all the tools and knowledge we need to COPE with them; but at the end of the day, if we stay in the same situation, we aren't addressing the core issue, we are pasting over the cracks.

I'm highly qualified to talk about this. As you can see from the introduction, I had the awareness to know that I was in a bad place and that if I didn't completely 'reboot' I would completely 'shutdown.' So I walked away from a very highly paid job to go travelling. I've done this a few times now. One of my ex-friends said to me (and he's the only person that's ever said this):

'You run away from your problems.'

That made me laugh out loud. Anyone that knows me knows I have never run away from anyone or anything. I'll ask you what I asked him: **'What takes more courage, staying in a job that is well paid and 'safe' but I am fully aware is destroying me, or venturing off into the complete unknown?'**

Am I telling you to walk away from a situation that is killing you? Absolutely! Will you get criticised? Probably, but remember, the source of criticism is usually envy.

> *Understanding stress takes intelligence and awareness, controlling stress takes courage. – Karl Rollison*

So...

QUESTION 2: 'STRESS: WHAT are you going to GIVE yourself permission to do about it?'

Stress Ninja says...

"See how important you are in the world?! You matter! People love you."

06. ATTACKED FROM ALL ANGLES

We travel to work on an overcrowded network or in congestion. We encounter rude people who think they are more important than we think we are. We are expected to work through our lunch breaks, stay late and be grateful. We are terrified of being sacked because we have a mortgage on a house we can't afford and loans on things we don't really need. We have a magic box that we carry everywhere. It allows us to stay in contact with each other, keeps us entertained and informed, allows us to take instant photos and share them with people we don't really know or like. This device is in itself a status symbol. This joy of being in constant contact with the world gets corrupted with work emails and calls from our bosses and colleagues 24 hours a day, so light joy becomes a heavy burden. We infect our homes with our work so it is no longer our sanctuary, there is no escape and there are no excuses. The once great 'there was no network coverage' or 'my battery died' are becoming less valid.

So we are at home with our partners whom we no longer communicate with because we sit there in silence looking from our phones, to our laptops, to our tablets to the television, and wondering why the relationship isn't working. Due to the long hours we don't get any exercise so we don't like what we see in the mirror. We don't have the time to cook so we eat processed food that is labelled low fat diet (but is actually full of salt, sugar, sweeteners and preservatives, and we wonder why we don't lose any weight). To numb the growing despair we open a bottle of wine and eat chocolate, whilst watching heavily processed, contrived 'reality' programs in an attempt to escape the nightmare that has become our lives. But it just makes it worse, because these programmes feature odious, self obsessed idiots who have bizarrely achieved celebrity status and who we subconsciously admire.

We then watch the News which is even more fabricated than the horrendous reality shows and soap operas we sit in front of. They tell us that our economy is on the brink of collapse, there is another global pandemic that will kill us all (though it never does) and that our lives are at risk due to the constant increase in terror attacks.

We go onto social media and see smiling people we know, don't know, sort of know, met once and /or hate, having an amazing life, and we don't realize that they are probably sitting at home thinking the same about us. Is it any wonder we are so stressed?

Before you say 'thanks for the summary, Karl, I thought you were supposed to be helping. Now I just feel worse', remember, from the first chapter, *scientia potentia est*, knowledge is power. Just keep reading, you are already taking control of your life. Stick with it. All will be explained.

WHAT IS BEING ATTACKED?

Have you ever been cold, wet and hungry? I bet you have, briefly. You know when you're getting ready for work, before breakfast on a cold dark winters morning and you've just stepped out of the shower. Isn't that a horrible feeling? Now imagine rather than wrapping up in a huge clean towel and walking into the warm lounge you are instead lying, shivering in a shop doorway with a damp piece of cardboard as a blanket and no options. Well, being warm, dry, sated and safe are basic, prime human needs that are hundreds of thousands of years old. There are many, many more, but these ones are by far the most important. In 1943 Abraham Maslow wrote a paper called the 'A theory of human motivation' in it he formulated 'Maslow's hierarchy of needs.' In this he identified a list of basic needs that a human being requires to be happy.

Very basically the original hierarchy is:

So, as you can see between our bosses and colleagues at work, our clients, our friends and family and (worst of all) the media and our 'friends' on social media, every aspect of our hierarchy of needs is under constant pressure of attack, from basic survival requirements up to achieving our peak achievements. Again, no wonder we're so stressed!

RUN AWAY!

Scary isn't it? Over the years I've heard a certain expression repeated by lots of people. I've heard it from multinational directors to housewives. I've heard friends say it and I bet even you may have used it, thought it or heard it from someone else...

'I wish I could just give everything up and go and live on a

remote desert island somewhere'

The reason people say and think this is because we know that this would be the polar opposite of all of previous negative descriptions and scenarios. They were all examples of varying degrees of fight or flight. There is a natural balance and equilibrium to all things.

At the other end of the scale there is rest and digest, or as I like to call it, *Chill & Heal....*

Stress Ninja says...

"You are being attacked everyday but I think you understand this now. It's not that scary when you know where, why and how, is it?"

07.   CHILL & HEAL

Rest and digest – (Scenario 3)

You are on one of the most remote islands of Fiji. The sky is the most perfect, deep blue you have ever seen. It is highlighted by the stunning turquoise of the sea. The water is so crystal clear, it looks good enough to drink. There is another island a few miles away, and during low tides you can walk over to it. The island is tiny and you can stroll around it in less than half an hour via the pure white sandy beach. There are no phones on the island, no mobile signal and definitely no Wi-Fi. There is only a handful of staff on the entire piece of land, and the few other people present are your friends. You feel totally safe and secure. You have just got back from the communal area where you have eaten a huge, freshly prepared lunch. The sun is smiling on the island but its hot rays are tempered by a cool breeze from the Pacific Ocean. You are lying, lazily swinging from side to side on a giant hammock suspended between two angled palm trees. Your partner is cuddled up next to you while you read one of your favourite books. One of the staff has put on the album you gave them. Two of your friends are on an adjacent hammock and they compliment you on your choice of songs. The music wafts over you complemented by the gentle rustle of the palm tree leaves and the background lapping of the water. One of the staff comes over to you and with a smile does the international hand gesture for 'drink?' You smile and give him the thumbs up. He chops a fresh coconut open with his machete then pours in some ice, some vodka and a couple of straws. You lie there with a smile on your face. Your stomach feels heavy and so do your arms and legs. You start to have some really great ideas about all the creative things you've been meaning to do. You have some amazing, innovative business ideas. You are so relaxed that your thoughts seem to merge with sleep causing an almost hallucinogenic state. You've got another month on this island. You let out a long deep sigh...

So what's happening here then?

- Your breathing has shifted, you are breathing out longer than you are breathing in. You are feeling totally satisfied, you are now slipping into the rest and digest response.

- Everyone is projecting love and positivity towards you. You are picking up on this energy and it creates a lovely synergy in the group.

- The island and Fijian staff has a lovely slow tempo and positive energy. Everyone is absorbing and projecting this. States are contagious, it's called sympathetic harmonic resonance, and under this influence it's almost impossible to experience stress.

- You feel safe and secure, your Adrenalin and Cortisol are low.

- You feel nice and heavy, your digestive and immune systems are running at 100%, your core is full of blood that has been diverted away from your arms and legs.

- You're stress is so low, your higher brain functions are kicking in and your creativity is firing. That is when you can formulate great ideas for the future. You are producing the hormone Dopamine.

- The voice of self doubt we all carry around in our head has been replaced with feelings of positivity and encouragement. This is confidence about the future.

- You are so relaxed, with your creativity and your intellect on full charge, that as you start to slowly drift off you have wonderful visions and hallucinations.

- Your levels of Oxytocin, Serotonin and Dopamine are highly elevated.

Sounds like heaven right? Of course it does. Well, believe me when I tell you that after a very short period, it isn't! How do I know? Well the seemingly idyllic scene above is an exact account of my own experience. Don't get me wrong. To start with it was paradise - being totally cut off and out of contact with the world, eating pancakes for breakfast, fish for lunch and dinner, sleeping in a mud hut. No water supply or electricity, having to bathe in the sea and carry a paraffin lamp at night. After a while all the things that made it beautiful were the very things that started to make it ugly. Seriously, how long would it be before you got the urge to leave the island? I planned on staying a month and only lasted 10 days!

This was research I did in the mid 2000's. I wanted to experience utopia. I reread my travel diary as research for this section of the book. This is what I wrote to summarise Fiji:

Even paradise feels like hell after a while. -Karl Rollison

So what am I getting at with all this? Remember when you were a kid and someone had a birthday party and you weren't invited? Maybe this has happened more recently? It doesn't matter anyway because it's the same feeling. It's the feeling of being excluded. We are pack animals and avoiding that feeling of rejection is part of our core programming. It's what makes us conform to the group and gives us social etiquette. If we feel excluded it will generate massive stress. However, listen...

There is no utopia. There is no paradise. There isn't supposed to be, not on Earth. These people you see on social media, and the celebrities you see on the news, aren't living the dream. They are just as insecure as you, probably more so. Everyone has problems. If you do your research you'll see that even winning the lottery is a curse. You are not missing out on the party. Acknowledgment of this fact gives a warm sense of inner peace and reduces stress.

BOREOUT – BE CAREFUL WHAT YOU WISH FOR.

Rest and digest just like fight or flight isn't supposed to be sustained. It is there for a specific purpose, in this case to shut down the body, process food, repair and replace cells and do some general housekeeping. Fight or flight leads to 'Burnout.' This is because we are overwhelmed by our environment, the environment being everything outside of the body.

Rest and digest can equate to feeling underwhelmed due to lack of external stimulation. We get out of sync with our surroundings this can cause an intense feeling of demotivation.

Lacking motivation can be a result of being over or under whelmed and is one of the worst feelings in the world. Our body will slip from growth to protection. To put it another way:

Burnout is when the challenge exceeds our ability. We will slip backwards into *PROTECTION.*

Boreout is when our ability exceeds the challenge. Again, we will slip backwards into *PROTECTION.*

ONE EXTREME TO THE OTHER

Want more proof of the effects of Boreout? What do large companies do if they want to get rid of a member of staff? Do they give them a massive amount of work to do and more responsibility? No, this could be seen as intimidation and bullying. No, they do the opposite. They take away their staff, status, and workload, so that all they do all day is surf the internet. It's a very clever yet sinister way to demotivate someone.

As with all my writings I try to include as much empirical information as I can- situations I have witnessed firsthand. Many years ago I worked in the same office as a really nice guy. Let's call him Paul. He was a quiet, inoffensive type that got excluded and overlooked for social gatherings.

I've always been interested in people's subtle body language. I would ask him about his garden and he would seem to grow physically, he would acquire some colour to his face and become animated in manner and speech. Then I'd ask him about work and it was like someone had pulled his plug. He would seem to deflate. So, he was completely out of his depth and should have been a gardener.

What happens when we feel overwhelmed? Our immune system is suppressed. We get sick. He would flit around the office wide eyed, sneezing, with a tissue perpetually held to his nose. Not a great look when dealing with clients. One day they got someone in to 'assist him.' This person was a sharp cookie and I knew exactly why he was there. Sure enough, as soon as he was up to speed, they promoted him above Paul.

Paul now felt betrayed by the company he had worked so hard for, but after a while he began to realise that he no longer had requirements and demands placed on him. He took advantage of his new freedom and began to use the time to research his beloved hobby and, for a brief period, the colour returned to his face, his posture improved and a spring could be seen in his step.

However, soon, when he realised that, unlike him, people didn't have time on their hands and no one else could afford to go for long lunches, he began to get out of sync with his environment. Worse still, he was out of sync with his colleagues. He felt excluded from the group. Over the next few weeks, the slumped, deflated and defeated demeanour returned. So too did the cold and flu symptoms. The only difference was that this time he wasn't wide eyed. He wasn't overwhelmed, he was underwhelmed. I had witnessed firsthand how his state had gone from Burnout through Flow and onto Boreout. Not a nice thing to see.

It must have been a very lonely situation. I mean, he couldn't even go to the doctors. What would he tell them? 'I've got no stress at work?' Imagine telling that to a GP who does 70+ hour weeks. Don't think you'll get much sympathy. So the only choice was to leave quietly. He shuffled off with a haunted look on his face. You must have seen that look, it's written on the face of every person who retires but is unsure of how to cope with the new set up.

It always surprises me when I speak to retired people who experience Boreout. Well, hello, it wasn't a surprise. You knew this would happen. You've known for the last 50 years in fact. You've had time to plan for it. You've had time to ask questions of yourself like, what do I really enjoy doing? This won't ever happen to you, not if you follow this book.

BTW: In the first 2 stress scenarios in *Chapter Two* did you notice the device used in the description? The two scenes should have depicted a grim picture. The scenario in this chapter should have painted a nice bright image. Did you notice the main difference though? In the first two it was written from the third person perspective or 'dissociated' (seeing yourself in the picture) where as the last one (scenario 3) was in the second person or 'associated' (looking from a personal perspective). I want you to acknowledge how powerful this is because we're going to be using it later on!

---

08.   WHAT'S THE ANSWER?

It's the same answer to a lot of things. It's one word. We need this if we want to get fit and still enjoy ourselves. We need this if we want to do well in our job and maintain a great social and family life. We need this type of diet if we want to stay healthy. This thing is so versatile it'll let us know how much money we've got and it'll even stop us falling over. It's...

BALANCE

If we are in a nice, safe, healthy environment and we are in good spirits, then we are in balance. To use the correct term in this situation, we are in 'Homeostasis.' We breathe in and out at the same rate. We are not in danger but were not bored either. We are actually generating a nice smooth sine wave. It is nice and even, with no spikes. So is this the ultimate state? Yes it is, but, being human, we have organic computers in our heads and these are analogue as opposed to the cold logic of a digital computer. Therefore nothing we do is ever truly on or off.

When it comes to experiencing a true optimum state we need to think of fight or flight and rest and digest as the two opposite ends of a scale. Our optimum state would float somewhere in the middle. The closer to the middle we get, the more desirable the state, this is known as the FLOW state..

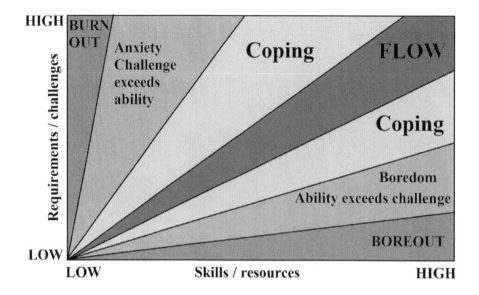

This is all very well but what does it mean in real terms? How do we know where we are on the above scale? How do we know how balanced we are? Wouldn't it be great to know how our stress levels are doing at any given time? Well, we could take regular samples of our saliva to measure the levels of Cortisol. We could also walk around all day hooked up to an Ambulatory Blood Pressure Monitoring device that takes constant, regular readings. However, there is a much easier way than that...

The Stress Meter

This is, as the name suggests, a gauge for measuring stress. We are going to be installing it in our heads. Don't worry, there is no surgery involved. In fact the gauge doesn't actually exist in any real sense, but it doesn't have to. It's the concept that's important.

Like any measuring device, what's important is accuracy. To build our gauge we first need to do some calibration. This is my favourite tool as a professional. I use it with all my clients and, like most really useful things, it's simplicity itself. I'll ask you the same question I ask them:

'How stressed do you feel right now? I want you to give me an exact number between 0 and 10. 0 would be halfway through a holiday of a lifetime and 10 would be being evicted from your home.'

This is exactly how I say it without any further embellishment or explanation.

What really amazes me is that, over the years, seeing clients all over the world, in all walks of life, I've never had anyone ask me to explain what I mean. They have never told me that they don't know or that the question confuses them. I just get a clear and precise number: 'I'm a 5 right now', 'I'm ok, I'm 2 and a half', 'I'm totally stressed... I'm an 8.'

As I mentioned before, the bio computers in our heads are analogue so it makes sense to have an old fashioned analogue gauge, like you would find on a boiler, but you can design yours however you want. You could just copy mine, here's what it looks like:

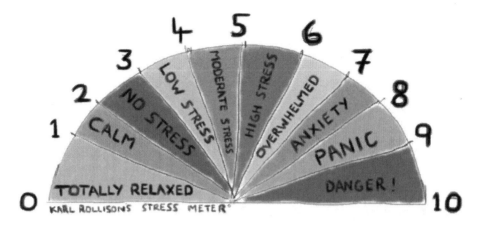

KARL ROLLISONS STRESS METER

This meter will take you a while to design but there's no rush and most people enjoy the process. I get my clients to carry the design around with them either on a piece of paper or on their phone and modify it as they go about their business. Most people are shocked just how much their stress levels vary throughout the day.

Please take this seriously and don't underestimate its power. You know my mantra by now 'Knowledge is Power.' You also know that to be a Ninja you need to understand your enemy. Well the enemy is stress and now you know what it looks like from your own perspective. Remember, it's not reality that changes the needle of our stress meter, it's our *perception* of reality. 10 people in a room could be experiencing the same thing but each person could have a different reading on their own gauge. If there were a massive snake in the room how would a professional snake handler's gauge look compared to someone with an extreme snake phobia?

So how do we install it? You already have. You are now aware of it, aware that we can monitor our own levels at any given time.

RECAP

OK so now you know the different types of stress. You know how dangerous stress can be and you know what it looks like from the only perspective that is relevant...yours.

Stress Ninja says...

"This stuff is SO easy once you decide that you want to step up and take control, just like you have!"

09.   THE RHYTHM OF LIFE

Isn't it great to now be fully aware of what our stress levels are doing at any given time? I see incredible, positive shifts in my clients once they install a stress gauge, and the same will happen with you. Be prepared to notice a strange and regular occurrence though. Throughout the day the needle on your gauge will suddenly drop for no reason. This is something that has been happening to you all your life, it's probably got you in trouble a few times, maybe you've found it terrifying at times. But once you know what it is, you'll see how wonderful it is (knowledge is power); and like a lot of our natural responses, it's there for your protection. It's called...

The ultradian rhythm

There is a rhythm and pulse to everything in the universe, tides, planets, seasons and, believe it or not, our brains. Every 90 minutes or so our brain activates a safety device that actually slows it down for 10 or 15 minutes. We probably know this as *Daydreaming*. Now that you know this, watch out for it. Know the amazing thing that I've discovered about this phenomenon? The busier and more focused we are (or are required to be) the deeper and more relaxing this feeling is. Think of it as a waveform. Think of it as balance.

The problem with this process is that people start to panic.

'Oh no! My brains stopped working just when I need it most!'

So what do people do? Have another coffee, knock back an energy drink, a high sugar snack or go and have a cigarette. However, with the external stimuli, guess what? Our stress levels rise and we start to produce Cortisol and Adrenaline. We then power up our Sympathetic Nervous system and slip into fight or flight. As previously explained, our higher brain functions then slow down or switch off, causing us to stop thinking, which leads to panic. A vicious circle! I have coined a phrase for this:

THE ULTRADIAN ULTIMATUM

The secret here is to recognise it, accept it and go with it. Think of this natural process as the wave pattern that it is. Then acknowledge the fact that you are being rewarded for your hard work. You can allow your eyes to close and you can switch off for 10 minutes. If you can't do this at your desk, then you can go to the toilet and sit in a cubical for 10 minutes. This is a really important thing to do, but it feels unnatural because of the high expectations placed on us today. I tell my clients the same thing that I tell my martial art students:

> If you don't want to end up broken physically or mentally, then listen to your body. It knows best! – Karl Rollison.

I explained the importance of going with the ultradian rhythms and shutting down for 10 minutes to one of my less enlightened clients. This guy was the head of his trading desk at a large city bank, and was so wrapped up in his own little world of self importance that he looked at me with indignation and said:

"What? I can't shut down for 10 minutes! Do you know how busy I am?"

"Oh, OK. Sorry. Who changes your colostomy bag? Do they do it at your desk?"

He looked horrified "I don't have a colostomy bag thank you! I go to the toilet like everyone else"

"WHAT!? You go to the toilet!? Don't you know how busy you are?"

I couldn't write about ultradian rhythms without telling you of the dangers of misreading this wonderful phenomenon. A few years ago someone I know mentioned, in passing, how they were reluctant to take the antidepressants they had just been prescribed by their doctor. I asked them what the problem was.

'I don't feel overwhelmed or anxious or anything. I just need to perform at work to a high level for a sustained period of time, and I keep losing focus. I don't know why. My doctor said it was a sign of stress'

I explained to them about the ultradian rhythm. They decided to postpone the drugs for a few weeks and go with the rhythm.

This person rang me up a week later and was pretty angry.

'I feel great Karl, I've been tuning into my natural rhythm. Now I've got consistent and sustained concentration, so I've cut back on sugar and caffeine. But answer me this: *Why the HELL aren't we told this stuff? Why am I being prescribed drugs? Why isn't this information more readily available?*'

I laughed, rubbed my head and said in a weary voice:

'*Because every time someone wakes up, takes responsibility for themselves and deals with their own problems, naturally, they are depriving the poor pharmaceutical companies of the revenue from the drugs that aren't being consumed!*'

Rant over.

You see, these rhythms are basically stepping up and taking control. They are actually lowering the frequency of our brains. The lower the frequency the more relaxed we feel. But here's the REALLY cool thing, we don't have to wait for these rhythms to cut in like a drunk waiting for a Pizza delivery, we can actually CHOOSE to lower them ourselves! Remember: knowledge is power, and the power of being a Stress Ninja is applying that knowledge. So I'll show you how in the next chapter

10. CHANGE YOUR RHYTHM

In the previous chapter I talked about the ultradian rhythm that come along and gently tell us that it's time to relax. But what is actually happening here? Well they are changing the FREQUENCY of our brains. I want to go over this quickly because it's nice to know. Knowledge is power, but what is more powerful is being able to do something about it.

Name	Frequency	Use
Beta	12 – 30 Hertz	This is the usual waking state of being. We experience this at work and when solving problems. You may be in this state right now, but it's not good to stay at this frequency for too long. If you follow the technique in this chapter, you won't be.
Alpha	7 – 12 Hertz	This is being awake but in a relaxed state of mind. This is the frequency we experience when we find ourselves daydreaming
Theta	4 -7 Hertz	This is a state of deep relaxation. This state can be accessed with good deep hypnosis or meditation. With practise we can access this frequency with the

Name	Frequency	Use
		technique in this chapter
Delta	0.5 – 4 Hertz	This is the slowest frequency that our brains can operate at. It is when we are in a deep, dreamless sleep. This can be accessed with meditation but usually requires years of training.

Give the following technique a try. You could record this into your phone and play it back or even get a friend to read it to you.

 Lowering your frequency

Find somewhere quiet where you won't be disturbed.

Lie or sit down and get as comfortable as possible.

Take a deep breath in and really fill your lungs. Pause and breathe out until your lungs are completely empty. Repeat this a few times.

Close your eyes and gently look up at the insides of your eyebrows.

Take a deep breath, hold it and scrunch up your eyes, clench your teeth, clench your fists, your buttocks and every muscle you can think of.

Breathe out and say 'ahhh' for the entire out breath whilst relaxing all of your muscles, keep your eyes closed and allow them to relax fully.

Focus on relaxing your jaw, (we use our jaws all the time and even tense them in our sleep, so it's nice to give them some time off).

Repeat the breathing a few times and, on the out breath, start to feel like you are sinking as your muscles feel heavier.

Now breathe normally. I want you to be aware of a beautiful, warm ball of light float down and entering into the crown of your head. You can feel the warmth of this light fill your body with positive energy. This will protect you wherever you go.

I want you to imagine a beautiful feather floating down, from side to side. There is no breeze and it is just gently falling.

Try to visualise the feather in as much detail as possible, see the individual follicles moving with the air movement. Get closer to it. Observe all the tiny details as it lazily sways from side to side. Get Closer still.

Now imagine you are the feather. Feel the nice, warm, safe sway of the feather as it continues on its journey.

The further down the feather floats the more you relax and the more you relax the further down it floats.

Do this for as long as you want. If you fall asleep that's fine, it's just relaxation. If you need to wake up for any reason, you will.

Just allow this experience to take you on a pleasant journey until you feel it's time to wake up.

Waking up

When you are ready, start to be aware of your surroundings and slowly begin to think about waking up. I want you to count back from 5 to 1 and when you reach 1, wake up and feel refreshed and energised.

5, Start to become aware of your body.

4, Feel the need to stretch out your muscles.

3, Allow your face to wake up and maybe have a yawn.

2, Come back into your surroundings.

1, Open your eyes.

You have just changed the frequency of your brain. You have wilfully done the same job as the ultradian rhythm. It's a fantastic feeling and it's free, but what upsets me is that most people never explore these wonderful, natural feelings and the only time they close their eyes is to sleep.

I will refer back to this technique later.

11. S.T.O.P / F.E.A.R

You now know that the ultradian rhythm is totally natural and is there for our protection. There is something else that we all have that is also there to protect us but, to be honest, it does too good a job and most of the time it does more harm than good. I call it...

S.T.O.P

This is an acronym I made up years ago to represent something that will try to hold you back all your life. It will keep you stuck in the same job. It will tell you you should be grateful for what you have. It will tell you you have a place and you shouldn't dare rise above that place. It will whisper that you are pathetic. It will shout that you are in danger when you are not. It will show you pictures of impossible and unlikely outcomes of your actions. It will try to convince you that you will end up alone, homeless and afraid. If it had its way you'd stay in your room and never go out. What is it? It can be known as self -talk, internal self-talk, internal dialogue and internal speech. Personally these are all too kind. I prefer...

Stupid Traumatising Overprotective Parent.

It's been there all of our lives and everyone has one. The difference between following our heart's desire and playing it 'safe' is how much we listen to our S.T.O.P. Me, personally, I listen to it too much sometimes. I feel myself becoming smaller and fearful of the outside world. Then, I remind myself who's in charge and I tell my S.T.O.P to shut the hell up!

> *Don't underestimate the S.T.O.P just because you haven't heard about it before. It has shaped mankind! People have done and are doing great things not because they haven't got a S.T.O.P but because they chose to ignore it. –Karl Rollison*

F.E.A.R

Our S.T.O.P is ultimately for our protection but it does such a good job it can prevent us from moving forwards. It does this by referencing our previous experiences and using them to generate potential outcomes for our actions.

> *'Remember when you tried that last time? You hurt yourself.'*
> *'You could never stand up and speak in public! Remember what happened at school?'*
> *'The last time you had a relationship it ended in disaster. Do you really want to take the risk again?'*

The mechanism the S.T.O.P uses to control us is the same one used by governments, dictators, some religions and generally bullies throughout history. It's fear. Or to use another one of my acronyms F.E.A.R – Future Events Aren't Reality.

If we walk down the street late at night and two seemingly normal people are walking towards us then our S.T.O.P has already created a F.E.A.R scenario in our heads, it will show us graphic images of being on the ground and them kicking and punching us. So we either overcompensate and start walking more aggressively or we close down and become a potential victim. What I'm saying is we have changed your physiology based entirely on our perception. In reality they walk past us without even being aware of our presence.

In Chapter 2 we talked about Pete. He may be great at his job but that's irrelevant. He has generated massive amounts of stress based mainly on his PERCPETION of his environment. The little voice in his head has convinced him that things are going to turn out badly for him. His S.T.O.P has generated F.E.A.R.

But Karl you said that our S.T.O.P and F.E.A.R are natural and are there for our protection. Aren't you being too harsh on them? No I'm not. Think back to all the opportunities you have missed out on in life, jobs, adventures, investments. Well, you have S.T.O.P and F.E.A.R to thank for that. These two things combined are more commonly known as... *WORRY*

Stress Ninja says...

"You are doing so well at all this. You now know that you truly are the one that holds the compass and decides the direction...no one else!"

12.   SLOW STRESS

I call worry "slow stress", but what is worry? Worry is the little voice in our head, presenting us with different scenarios via words or picture about some outcome, which, let's face it, will probably never happen. These two things generate consistent and sustained negative emotions. To give it its technical name, "Chronic Stress". To give it its more common name - worry. I'm going to share a **Scroll of Enlightenment** with you now coz we're mates. To save confusion I will contextualise the stats (proven stats I might add) into real terms, so pay attention:

Take 100 people in any part of the world with a mixture of worries (I'm talking about everyday issues here not terminal illness or death). Imagine these people biting their nails and lying awake at night. Now, out of these 100 people 88 of them will never encounter their worry. It just never materialised. Out of the 12 people that did meet their woes 9 people said it wasn't anywhere near as bad as they thought it would be. Of the remaining 3 people 2 said that they wouldn't have changed anything because it was such a great lesson.

> *Remember, we learn more from one disaster than from a thousand successes! – Karl Rollison*
>
> So, anyway, out of the 1 person in 100 who said that the situation they feared was as bad as they thought it would be, in retrospect, all admitted that not only was it a great lesson but it made a great story to tell others.

I've had a lot of worry in my life, most of which never happened.
– Mark Twain

On the other hand, worry can be quite life affirming. It makes us live in the moment. What about a worry about something in the future and it dominates our thoughts 24 hours a day 7 days a week? The deadline is getting closer. There isn't even escape when we sleep (when we CAN sleep). Suddenly we are in the situation we have been dreading, the situation that has ruined our lives for the last few months. The funny thing is that as soon as the situation became actualized and we were in the middle of it we stopped worrying. Then, before we know it we are out the other side. I'm sure we've all felt this, then what? There is a small moment of relief, and then there is a void. Suddenly we don't have a purpose anymore, no drive. That worry actually gave us some drive and motivation.

There are three really important questions about worrying:

1.   Am I in danger?

2.   Do I have to deal with this issue right now?

3.   Will anyone get hurt if I don't deal with this?

This makes you stop and enjoy the moment. I think impending moments make life more interesting. Like your last few days of a fantastic holiday. In my opinion these are the best; you start living in the moment and stop taking your surroundings for granted, fully aware that it will all soon be over.

Right, now, pay attention. Of the following tasks, I want you to choose the one that is most UNCOMFORTABLE - the worst thing you could imagine. Chose one:

1. Do a speech in front of 100 guests at a black tie event

2. Run a marathon

3. Climb a rock face

4. Pick up and handle a spider, rat, snake

Have you chosen one? Good. Now I want you to imagine that you have given your guarantee that you will complete this task in the next two months.

What happened to your S.T.O.P? I bet it's gone into overdrive right?' 'You can't do that you'll die.' 'You'll look stupid. People will laugh.' 'You'd have a heart attack.'

Now, you know this already but, how does the S.T.O.P manifest itself? Does it show you pictures or does it prefer to torment you with noises?

Is your S.T.O.P a voice? Is it your voice? Is it one of your parents? Perhaps it's an old teacher.

Where is your S.T.O.P? Some people tell me it's behind their head. Some say it's inside their head. Some say that it feels like a whisper in their ear. Maybe it's a clear vivid picture right in front of your eyes.

You get the picture. Now I want to show you HOW to control it!

 STOP the S.T.O.P – turning off the little voice with aggression

Wherever your annoying unhelpful internal little voice is, turn around to it or picture yourself turning around to it, and treat it the same as a person who is trying to hold you back for their own gain, perhaps a boss, a teacher, a parent. Screw up your face and say in the most aggressive, menacing and angry voice you can possibly muster:

'You don't control me! I CONTROL YOU! I've been listening to your rubbish for far too long! I can do what I want, when I want so SHUT THE HELL* UP!!!'

I want you to imagine your S.T.O.P cowering away from you because for the first time in its existence it has firstly, been acknowledged, and then firmly put in its place.

*add the expletive of your choice

Now, how good and empowering does that feel?

If you are a totally non aggressive person then there is another, quieter technique for you to try.

STOP the S.T.O.P – the 'Shhh' technique

The 'shhh' noise is very powerful. Try this, next time you are in a noisy room and you want to get everyone's attention. Rather than trying to shout over the noise, simply make a long 'shhh' noise. I saw a little, old Japanese instructor quietly do this in the Budokan (a massive training arena dedicated to martial arts in the centre of Tokyo) and 300 noisy chattering people instantly stopped and paid attention. I don't know if it's part of our core programming to do with danger, and perhaps snakes, but this works!

Another thing I've been told on my travels is that the 'shhh' noise is common in all cultures regardless of language. Even remote tribes naturally use this to quieten babies. It's been used since the beginning of time. One theory is that it's the noise that blood makes as it pumps through the body, as heard by the foetus. I don't usually include stuff that I can't prove, but regardless of the origins there is one thing I do know, the following technique works:

 <u>STOP the S.T.O.P – turning off the little voice with harmony</u>

Think of all your worries and woes. This works really well at night, and I know people that have used this to help with insomnia.

Get comfortable. Take a really deep breath in, pause then breathe out for a long time. Repeat.

Then close your eyes, take a deep breath in and on the exhale make a 'shhh' noise. This could be a series of short 'shhh' or a long 'shhhhhhh' one will feel better than the other, you decide.

After a very short time your mind will quieten.

As you do this technique try to think of all the things that bother you. I bet you can't!

The other cool thing is that you should be aware of your muscles relaxing as you do it. Some people find it better if they imagine a loved one doing the 'shhh.'

The other thing is, using our imagination. Remember, most of the techniques in this book can work just as well imagining doing them as opposed to actually doing them. So if we need to do this in public, on a train, or a bus or at work just *imagining* doing it should be just as affective, although this takes a bit of practise.

WORRY DOWNLOAD

So we have been tossing and turning all night with things rattling around in our head. I've had lots of clients with this issue and, as usual, an effective solution is pretty simple. Download it. How? Write it down. Write down everything that is bothering you and make an action list. Simple. They say a problem shared is a problem halved, well most of the time we don't want to burden people with our worries, but this is just as effective.

Reframing - Putting things into perspective

I love reframing because it fits with my method of coaching, simplicity. We do it all the time. If someone comes to us with an issue, chances are they are stuck and are not viewing it from different angles. Or to use a cliché, 'can't see the wood for the trees.'

He sat opposite me and you didn't have to be an expert to see he was preoccupied:

'Every time I see an email from my boss I get a sinking feeling. Every time he talks to me, I read something else into it. I'm just convinced they are going to sack me.'

'So what? You'll get a payoff and do something you want to do.'

'No, I'll lose everything. I won't get another job.'

'OK. So I want you to imagine that you have been feeling ill for a while and you have been to the doctors. He rings you to tell you that your results are back and to come into the surgery immediately. How would that feel?'

'My god! That would be the worst thing ever.'

'Ok, so imagine that you are going to go to the doctors after work, so you keep yourself busy in the day. What would be going through your mind?'

'Cancer and death!'

'OK. Really think about it. Imagine sitting at your desk and feeling that oppressive hollow feeling of despair. Suddenly your boss rings you and asks you to come into his office. Would you be sacred?'

Of course not, I'm gonna find out that I'm going to die. Who cares about the job?'

'Your mobile is facing down on the desk and it starts ringing. It is either your boss or your doctor. Which would you prefer it to be?'

'My boss. Why would the doctor be ringing me? To tell me to get to him earlier? That would probably mean I have hours to live.'

'Ok so you're at the doctor's and you're about to knock on the door. He calls you in and asks you to take a seat. How would you feel?'

'I'd be terrified.'

'How would this compare to sitting opposite your boss?'

He looked at me like I'd just told him I loved him, 'Absolutely no comparison.'

'Right now think about your job. Are you worried anymore?'.

'No, not at all.' He laughed and looked relieved with a hint of confusion, always a good sign. Job done!

He then surprised me by asking what the doctor said.

I just shrugged. It was my turn to look confused, why does that matter? I thought.

'Oh...I don't know, er, I suppose he said you were pregnant or something'

So whatever it is you are worried about, really take it to the extremes with explosions and people running and screaming. Really let your imagination run wild. Then think about your problem again. Is it really that bad?

THE WORRIED TIME TRAVELLER

Think back to a period of your life where you had a problem. A period where perhaps you had a health issue, financial issues, redundancy, relationship strife or maybe a combination of all of these. Remember how you felt at the time? How did it turn out? Were the sleepless nights, anxiety and anger worth it? When the situation came to its conclusion, did it justify all that worry? Of course it didn't.

If you could travel back in time what would you say to your younger self? Something like: "It probably feels like you're caught in the middle of a storm at the moment and you feel trapped but you DO come out the other side. Things aren't ANY WHERE NEAR as bad as you think they are!"

You could probably apply this to every worry you've ever had, I know I can.

 Future Self Advice.

Now, I want you to close your eyes and think about what you are going through right now. Think about all the negative effects this anxiety is having on your life. Think about the time you lie awake at night thinking about it. Think about how it affects your mood. Think about how much time this negative self talk (S.T.O.P) takes up. How unproductive it is?!

Now, as you sit there, I want you to imagine a flash of light in the room and your future self is in there. Imagine what you look like and what you are wearing. See how healthy and fit you look. Then with a big warm smile I want your future self to say:

"Listen, I know it feels like there is no way out from this but I'm your future self and I am here to tell you that everything works out well. There's nothing to stress about. Stop worrying. Everything is OK and you're going to be just fine!"

The thing about worry and problems is that if we just look at them from another angle it makes them more manageable. This is why we usually feel better when we've spoken to someone else about the issue, they can make us see it in a different way. Sometimes looking at a problem from a higher perspective works really well. Think about a time you were in a whirlwind of worry. Think back to that feeling. Perhaps something happened that, at the time seemed like a drastic situation. Perhaps at the time you felt it was the end of our world, maybe you were sacked from a job. Perhaps you had split up with a partner. The reality is that when we look from a different angle, in this case backwards, we see that these are usually the things that define us.

The problem is we don't tend to think of things this way when we are in the middle of them. Whatever problems we have right now will pass and we'll get through them. We never know what the outcome will be, but we usually presume the worst. Here's a little fable that I love. I read it myself if I'm in the middle of a storm and I send it to friends, family and clients if they are struggling. It's a Taoist fable that could well be over 2000 years old but it's just as relevant today as it was then.

It's the story of a simple farmer and his horse:

One day his horse runs away. His neighbours come over to commiserate, saying, "We're so sorry about your horse." And the farmer says "Who knows what's good or bad?" The neighbours are confused because this is clearly terrible. The horse is the most valuable thing he owns. The horse comes back the next day and he brings with him 12 feral horses. The neighbours come back over to celebrate, "Congratulations on your great fortune!" And the farmer replies again: "Who knows what's good or bad?" And the next day the farmer's son is taming one of the wild horses and he's thrown and breaks his leg. The neighbours come back over, "We're so sorry about your son." The farmer repeats: "Who knows what's good or bad?" Sure enough, the next day the army comes through their village and is conscripting able-bodied young men to go and fight in war, but the son is spared because of his broken leg. And this story can go on and on like that. Good. Bad.

Who knows?

So what's the answer? Well, we need to switch off the whirlwind of information in our head. How? It's the basis of most spiritual teachings, meditations, Yoga and martial arts around the world throughout history. It's LIVING IN THE PRESENT.

See nothing has ever happened in the future! Nothing! No man has ever achieved any great things in his past or his future, everything that has ever happened or ever will happen, happens in the present.

Everything we do is in the NOW! We can *PLAN* to do things in the future and USE our *PAST* experience to do the task, but we can only ever do anything in the PRESENT. So think about it logically, how can we dedicate ourselves to doing something 100% unless we just focus 100% on what we are actually doing? We can only do this by switching off the future and shutting down the past. This is what is known as the state of FLOW. I'm now going to show you, what I consider to be *one of the most powerful techniques there is...*

Stress Ninja says...

"I know you are starting to feel it...that amazing sensation of having control over your life!"

13.   NO MIND

The doubt and anxiety I always experienced before I entered the Dojo was outweighed by the sensation of relief, excitement and pride I felt afterwards. It was the middle of summer in a little community hall on a rough council estate in East London. We sat in a semi circle around Tony whilst we rehydrated and warmed down after a heavy training session. Tony was, in my opinion, just what a true martial artist should be. He was kind, calm, funny, approachable and friendly. People relaxed in his company and he had the ability to make everyone feel good about themselves - in other words, he was a gentleman.

He also had great awareness, balance, flexibility, an encyclopaedic understanding of body dynamics and bio mechanics, was strong but never used strength, and of course he was diamond tough. He was also uber cool. The type of cool that you either have or you don't, you can't fake it. If he was in a restaurant and someone found a bomb, and everyone was knocking over tables and screaming to the exit, Tony would have walked out quietly, after finishing his meal and paying for it, leaving a generous tip.

'Tony, can I ask you a question?'
'Yeah course you can'

'Have you always been so calm and cool?' He looked slightly embarrassed by his own question.

Tony let out a laugh, took a mouthful of water and shook his head smiling. He screwed the lid back on the water bottle and cleared his throat. 'When I was a kid I nearly died a few times from severe asthma attacks. They were brought on by stress. As a kid I had a lot of stress. Everyone thought, because I was skinny with glasses, that I must have been clever, but I missed so much school that I was actually a bit thick, which meant I got more stressed so I had more time off school. As I got older and more self aware, I decided to embark on a mission to control and master my stress. I didn't have access to any counselling or therapy so, I did what millions of people have done before me throughout history, I turned to martial arts. As you all know, if you think that martial arts have all the answers to all of your problems, then you are absolutely right! After years of study I still get stressed, but I can control it and it hasn't affected my health since I was a bullied, downtrodden, vulnerable kid.

'So how do you give off this presence you have, total calm and in control with a slight air of menace?'

'I don't think...'

Everyone was leaning forwards knowing that we were on the verge of finding out about this mysterious man. **I don't think** it's any of your business? **I don't think** I should tell you? **I don't think** you'd understand? What was he going to say?

He sat there taking another gulp of water then remained silent. I couldn't resist.

'Sorry... You don't think WHAT?'

98

'No, that's it,' he said with a smile. 'I don't think.'

He placed the bottle next to him, crossed his legs and folded his arms. 'Look guys, this is about as hard a training as you could get. You all turn up 3 times a week and I respect all of you for that.'

I could vouch for that statement, in the last year I had cracked 3 ribs, broken a finger, chipped a tooth, got knocked out, choked out and would even throw up on occasions. Once inadvertently splashing Tony's brand new trainers... I think, coincidently, that was the day I got knocked out.

'The only way we could make this even more realistic is if I just attacked you without warning, but then we'd be in an 'Inspector Clouseau and Cato' situation and that would involve me hiding in your house waiting for you to come home from work before jumping out of your linen basket, but sorry, I just don't have the time!

'So as far as we can (in a controlled environment) we have cultivated a realistic approach to martial arts.' He then looked at Adam who had started at the same time as me. 'Ad, do you remember your first lesson? I said I was going to attack you at full speed with full power and you had to respond. What did you do?'

'I panicked! I thought it was going to be like Karate where I knew what the attack was going to be, where I was to be hit. When you said, "just respond" I tensed up.'

'What went through your mind? Do you remember?'

'Yeah, of course I do. I remember thinking about getting hurt. Then I thought about going to hospital and I had a vision of ringing my boss and telling him I wouldn't be in.'

'What else?'

'Well, it was my first lesson. I thought other people would be judging me. I retraced my conversations with you before I joined. Had I given you the impression that I was a Karate expert? Did you think I was something I wasn't? Was the room full of martial arts experts and boxers? Was this some form of Fight Club? Is it OK to mention Fight Club?'

'Do you remember what happened next?'

'Yes, you shook my hand and asked me to sit down.'

'Yes, because I was playing with your adrenaline. I wanted to see if you had any arrogance. I was testing to see if you were nice, humble and friendly, or if I'd have to ask you to leave.'

Tony stood up and waved his finger around the room. 'If I ask any of you to stand and face me and I tell you I'm going to attack you what happens?'

I decided to pipe up, 'It's a weird feeling, everything seems to change somehow. I don't acknowledge anyone else in the room, time slows down and my vision changes.'

'But what goes through your mind?'

'Nothing'

'Exactly, you don't think! In Japan it's called mushin or "no-mind". I've watched all of you change since you've been training. First you only had mushin when you were in front of me. Then you had it with each other, now I can see it as you walk into the Dojo. You know why you have mushin?'

We all looked at each other with furrowed brows.

'Because, what are the alternatives? None of you are psychic. You can't pre-empt what my attack will be. There are thousands of ways I could attack you. So to keep you safe the conscious mind steps back and lets the wise one, the UNCONSCIOUS mind, take over. Your body and mind become one without the time lag and delay of having to consult the conscious mind. It knows to shut up. You get slammed straight into the moment, into the here and now.

'I just flow in life. I don't think, I respond. I live as a Taoist. I live in the moment. I never dwell on the past and I'm not intelligent enough to pre-empt the future. You just need to have faith that your unconscious mind has all the answers and it will look after you.

'Now, there are thousands of possible attacks in this false, controlled arena, but having mushin keeps you safe.' He then threw a thumb over his shoulder, and leant forward slightly, his tone changed in order to deliver the next bit with more gravity (It worked). 'That out there isn't a controlled environment and there are trillions and trillions of potential situations that could present themselves. Yet, we worry and stress over things we have no control over. Your mission is to cultivate that feeling of mushin, not outside the door of this Dojo, not when you face me, but when you open your eyes in the morning!'

The Overprotective voice in our heads will hold us back. The little warm feeling in our stomachs will lead us forward. Turn down the volume of the voice and tune into the feeling. This is your instinct, your intuition, your friend and it'll never let you down. – Karl Rollison

If you want to experience the feeling of mushin, or no-mind, and just flow with life then practise the following techniques. I think they are amongst the most powerful techniques we have at our disposal.

 ## ONE POINT TECHNIQUE

Stage one

When you first do this technique try to do it when you are feeling a bit stressed, perhaps after work or a commute. I want you to note what number your stress gauge is showing.

Do this with a partner if you can, and perhaps get them to read this out to you, or record it yourself and listen to it. You could just read it, it doesn't matter, you'll find what works for you.

OK If you can, do this in a quiet place with someone you know. Before you start think of a colour that you love, a warm positive, empowering colour. Now think of a colour you dislike. First off, stand still with your feet shoulder width apart and get your partner to gently push your shoulders from the front and the back. Make sure they remember how much power they use. Notice how you move in response to the push. Then walk around the room, notice how you feel but ask your partner to observe how you move.

Take a few deep breathes and concentrate on the pause between the in and out breath.

I want you to imagine you're a tree with branches growing out of your head. These branches are your thoughts. Some are your future thoughts others are past thoughts, past regrets, future anxieties perhaps? Only you will know how many there are and how big they are. Look up and see the branches. Close your eyes.

I want you to place one hand with the palm facing your stomach a few inches in front of (but just below) your belly button. Now place the other hand with the palm facing the back of your other hand a few inches away. Stay like this for a while and notice the heat from your hands and focus your attention to that area. Now slowly rotate your hands around each other. Try both directions, one way will feel good and the other way won't, this is ALWAYS the case.

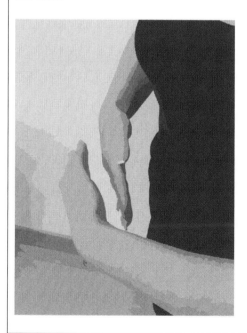

As you move your hands around each other imagine you are wrapping a thread around your hands. This imaginary thread goes into the area below your navel and is connected (via pulleys) up to the branches on your head, your worries, anxieties and fears. As you move your hands feel heat generate below your belly button. Breathe at a nice even pace. The more thread you wrap around your hands the more your branches retract.

As you breathe in imagine you are breathing in your favourite colour through the top of your head as well as your mouth. As you breathe out, breathe out the colour you dislike.

Breathe in positive energy and breathe out the negatives. See the bad colour leave your mouth taking negative thoughts, feelings and energy with it.

I want you to imagine that the thread around your hands is your favourite colour and it feels warm and comfortable. When you feel that you no longer have branches, stop spinning your hands and allow them to rest below your belly button. Focus on that area. Imagine a warm glow there.

Now breathe at a normal pace, nice colour in, bad colour out. With your eyes closed imagine you no longer have branches.

See the warm glow below your belly button. Feel the heat and acknowledge that it also has a certain weight to it. It feels nice and secure. What number is your stress gauge showing now?

Stage 2

Now place your hands at your sides and as you breathe out see roots growing from your fingers in your favourite colour. Watch as they leave your hands and fingers and connect with the floor.

Now see roots growing from the tops of your thighs and make their way into the ground. Every time another root goes into the ground feel it pull you down slightly. Feel your legs get slightly heavier. See roots growing from below your navel and connecting to the ground. Each time a root touches the ground feel the weight, and feel how it connects you to the ground.

See the biggest, brightest glowing roots of your favourite colour going down into the ground and off into the distance as far as you can imagine.

See and feel these roots growing from your body into the ground. Now imagine these beautiful roots weaving off into the distance. Feel the warmth and weight of your belly button. Keep imagining these roots until you are aware of a heavy sensation in your legs.

The way to test if you have done this properly is to open your eyes and walk around the room. You should feel heavy. If you did this with a partner get them to give you a gentle push as they did at the beginning of the technique. You should stand firmer and be harder to move.

This may seem a little involved but, with practice, it will take you no time to get this feeling. You don't have to follow this to the letter, experiment. The important thing is that heavy, solid feeling. Try to feel anxious or worried in this state. I bet your stress gauge is pretty low now right?

Below is another, less involved version of One Point. Do this technique at a different time from the one above, to get a clear indication of their effectiveness.

 ## One Point – the Mountain

I've done this with my students for years. It works especially well after a workout.

Make a note of your stress gauge. Lie or sit down in a comfortable quiet room. Focus on your breathing and notice the pauses. Feel your muscles relax and allow your jaw to relax.

If you have done other relaxation techniques in this book, you'll know what works for you. Do one now. When you are feeling relaxed imagine you are an eagle flying over trees under a beautiful clear blue sky. Feel the cool fresh air fluttering your wings. Look down and see your sharp talons. Hear the echo of your cry as you rule the sky.

I want you to see a mountain in the distance. It's a beautiful sight and it dominates the landscape. Visualise yourself flying towards it. Every beat of your wings allow you to relax even more. Take as long as you want to reach the mountain. You want to be as relaxed as possible.

Now, see the mountain below you. Slowly swoop down and land on its tip. Feel the rock underneath your claws. Now look around and see how small everything looks from this vantage point. Slowly feel yourself sinking into the mountain. As you sink down allow yourself to relax even more. Eventually you realise that you are the mountain. Look around you. You are the most powerful thing on earth. Your base goes through the earth. You are part of the earth. You are immovable. Just imagine how you feel as a mountain. See your base disappear in every direction into the distance.

When you are ready, get up and move around. You should feel nice and heavy. Try to get anxious in this mindset. What is you stress gauge reading now?

And finally this is the One Point method I use all the time. I use it whenever I feel myself getting angry. This quickly dissolves anger. It takes practise. As with all this stuff, there is no right or wrong. It's whatever works for you.

One Point – the ground grab

Note your stress gauge. You can be in any position for this, but I usually do it standing. Imagine a network of thick roots of your favourite colour a few feet below the ground, and they disappear off in all directions into infinity. Now imagine you have an invisible, powerful, giant hand that protrudes from below your belly button but is connected to the branches of worry from your head. Now imagine that the hand thrusts down into the ground and firmly grabs hold of one of the thick roots and pulls in the branches at the same time. Anchoring you firmly to the planet. Feel the pull from the earth. That's it. What's the reading on your gauge now?

No matter what the issue my clients have, I can usually sort it out by showing them how to do the One Point. Over the years this technique has helped people with creative blocks, anxiety and panic attacks, to mention just a few. Using this technique I've helped many people completely and calmly overcome ANY phobia. When used in martial arts it turns off the pre-emptive instinct, so instead of trying to read the opponent's actions, which leads to tensing up and potential injury, they simply relax, flow and respond. Imagine being in that mindset all the time. With practise, you can be.

14.   QUICK STRESS

By following this book so far we can now monitor our stress levels at anytime using our stress gauge. If the needle creeps up we can do a technique to nudge it back down. The One Point technique from the previous chapter can bring down the overall blanket level of our stress. Our main enemy is our production of Cortisol when things get challenging, this is known as the stress hormone. To counteract this we can wilfully produce Oxytocin, the love hormone. They have a very close relationship, as one goes up the other comes down. I'm going to show you some quick techniques to deal with acute stress such and anxiety, anger, phobias etc; things that may pop up out of the blue and need to be dealt with quickly and quietly. Anger is the sharp end of stress and we need to deal with it as soon as it appears. If we don't we are in danger of losing control. We have a saying in Ninjutsu:

How can you expect to control your opponent if you can't control yourself?

ANGER

Think about something that makes you angry. Maybe it's a situation or a person. Maybe it happened recently or ages ago, it doesn't matter. Really try to imagine the situation.

Now, have you noticed what happens to your hands? Your fists clench. This is a natural manifestation of angry thoughts. You see, if you can't clench a fist then you can't get angry. Don't believe me?

Think about that angry situation again.

Pressure Release:

Open your dominant hand in front of you with you palm facing you and stretch out your fingers. With the other hand form a pincher and pull down the little finger of your hand.

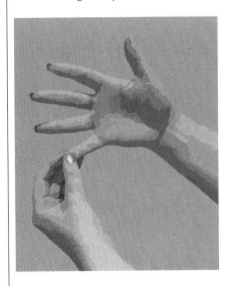

Now, think of that situation again. I bet you can't get angry now can you?

It also uses a martial arts technique that derives from the art of Jin Shen Jutsu where different fingers relate to different parts of your bodies meridian network, and thus different emotions. It is a form of meridian therapy. Trust me, this stuff works. In Ninjutsu we work on meridian points (Kyusho points) to cause damage when they are struck, but they can also heal when massaged.

I doubt that you are sceptical about this because you are obviously an open minded, intelligent person, otherwise you wouldn't have this book in your hand, but I had a client once who shook their head and laughed at the mention of meridian manipulation.

'Have you heard of acupuncture?' I asked

'Heard of it? I've actually had it done. I damaged my shoulder and after different things failed to work I was referred to acupuncture.

'Did it work?

'It was amazing'

'Well the first documented use of acupuncture was around 198BC. Yet up until the 1970s it was considered Witchcraft in the West. Now it's widely accepted by the medical community. This is exactly the same thing but without needles.'

He apologised for laughing. That client now successfully uses this all the time.

111

ROAD RAGE

I have a theory about road rage. As we said before, it's almost impossible to experience anger if we can't form a fist. Now, there is a direct correlation between our bodies and our thoughts and vice versa.

However, the problem is that when we are driving or pushing a shopping trolley or standing on a packed train or bus holding onto a hand rail, what are we doing with our hands? We are forming fists. We are effectively telling our brains that its anger time.

Next time you get angry in your car I want you to try this.

!!!ONLY DO THIS IF YOU FEEL IN CONTROL OF THE CAR!!!

 Finger spread:

It's very simple really, just loosen your grip on the wheel. Open your hands a little and grip the steering wheel with your thumb and palm rather than strangling in with all your fingers. You will find that this dramatically reduces stress and anger.

Now, I want to build on the technique at the top of this chapter. Obviously, you can't do this when driving, but later on I'll show you a version you can use.

<u>The Hissing finger:</u>

I want you to do the hand technique at the top of the chapter again. This time, as you pull the little finger down, I want you to imagine that all the anger and stress in your body is escaping from a valve between the little finger and the ring finger. As you do this I want you to make a hissing noise like escaping air. The noise you make should be from your mouth but pushed out from your stomach. You know the noise a tyre makes when you let the air out? It starts of high pressure, fast and high pitched and as it empties the pitch drops and slows.

As with most techniques, the times they really work are when you need them most. This is a really powerful system.

Now, what is your least favourite colour? A colour you dislike in a gas form. I want this colour to represent something you don't like. For example, I love the colour green but if I think of green gas it's repulsive.

So, if you experience anger whilst driving...

The gas release valve:

Loosen your grip on the steering wheel if it's safe to do. Extend the little finger of your dominant hand and imaging air escaping from the base of your little finger and let out a long deep hissing noise. I want you to imagine a plume of the horrible coloured gas and feel all the tension and anger drain from the top of your heads to the tips of your toes. I think you'll be amazed how well this works. One of my clients told me that this techniques works so well for him that he has to wind the window down to let out the gas.

You can pull your little finger down and I guarantee no one will bat an eyelid. As for the gas escaping, well you can breathe out and **imagine** seeing the gas escaping and **imagine** hearing the hissing as the gas escapes.

Anxiety.

This is something that needs to be reduced as soon as it is registered. Here are some great techniques that continue on from the above.

SPEECH!

Another really cool application of the **Gas Release Valve Technique** is

when doing a speech or presentation. After all, public speaking is the

NUMBER 1 phobia in the world. If you don't know why this is in a section

about quick stress, then you've obviously never been asked to 'say a few

words.' I've helped lots of clients with this technique. Think about it. It

actually looks really natural when you do it, like you are just gesticulating with

your hands, but you're actually releasing the tension and anxiety.

This is very simple. People try to make all of this complicated but it

doesn't have to be. If you want to generate Cortisol then take on too much

work, eat processed food, drink alcohol and caffeine, don't exercise, hide

away from your responsibilities and eat loads of sugar. If you want to do the

opposite there are two fantastic, natural methods to generating Oxytocin, you

can modify your breathing or you can stimulate your skin, through a caress or

a cuddle. *Your skin and your lungs are the two ways you interact with*

your environment.

Anyway, here is another really cool technique to very quickly drop your levels of Cortisol by raising your Oxytocin, this is good for all forms of stress but it can be used as a quick calming technique.

 Calmer -<u>The Figure of 8 technique:</u>

Tap on the centre of your forehead between your eyebrows with your middle finger about 10 times. Now take a really deep breath in, hold it for a second and breathe out until your lungs are completely empty. Breathe normally and (if appropriate and safe) close your eyes, gently scribe a sideways figure of '8' on your forehead. Take up the entire forehead with this eight. With your eyes still closed imagine you can see the movement of the 8 through your forehead. Do it in a nice smooth rhythm with a nice gentle pressure. That's it! This has been proven to promote Oxytocin. I know one thing, it works amazingly well and it makes me feel fantastic. I also have a lot of positive feedback from all my clients.

As I've mentioned a few times, we have inbuilt mechanisms to deal with our issues. Our bodies have the answers without having to reach for medication. I've already mentioned meridian techniques. What do kids do when they are anxious or need reassurance? They suck their thumb. The thumb is linked to anxiety. However, when it comes to stress defence, particularly self defence, it's probably not a great idea to start sucking your thumb. There is a simple alternative.

 The Thumb Anxiety reducer

Spread the fingers of your dominant hand out.

Clamp the thumb with the other hand in a pincer motion. Don't grab it with your fist, remember what we said earlier.

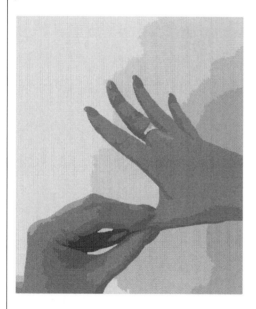

Hold this for about 90 seconds.

You should suddenly notice a change in your anxiety.

Do it for as long and as often as necessary. You can't overdose on this stuff.

I cured a chronic elevator phobia with this one technique.

OK, there is a situation where everyone, no matter who it is, is more susceptible to anxiety, stress, anger, hate or any other negative emotion. It's when we are tired. Guess what? There is a great natural remedy for that too. Try this next time you are tired.

 WAKE UP - Alternate Nasal breathing

I was first shown this by a Yoga expert in Ubud, Bali - the Yoga capital of the world. It's a form of Pranayama or breath control. As I understand it, it realigns the energies in our bodies and brings the left and right hemispheres of the brain into alignment. It also de-stresses and revitalises. Some of my clients have reduced, or even given up, caffeine by using this method.

REMEMBER, as with any breathing exercise, S.T.O.P if you get dizzy.

Cover your right nostril with your right thumb, keep the other finger straight and out of the way, to not restrict the airflow. Take a deep, long breath in. Pause.

Cover your left nostril with your left thumb, fingers up, and breathe out fully through your right nostril. Pause. Then cover your right nostril again and breathe in through your left nostril as before. Keep this cycle of left and right going. Try 10 times on each nostril. You should be aware of a shift in your energy levels, like a caffeine rush.

OK, LET RECAP THE BOOK SO FAR:

We already have a natural stress management system, the ultradian rhythm. We just don't listen to it. Now we know it's there we can.

How can we cope with stress if we can't identify and quantify it? That's where the stress gauge comes in.

When we transfer the stress gauge into our head we change our relationship with stress.

We should now realise that we don't HAVE to be a victim of our own responses. We can and will take control. We are taking control.

The sharp end of stress is anger. We can experience massive stress, but still control ourselves. If we experience extreme anger we lose control.

What good is having a really sensitive stress monitor if we can't actually do anything about it? This is where relevant, powerful techniques come into play.

Stress Ninja says...

"Imagine how much more prepared you now are for ANY of life's challenges. You have a sort of virtual Swiss Army Knife of techniques that you can carry anywhere. People are really going to start noticing the difference...you'll see!"

15.   CAUSE AND EFFECT

So, throughout this book we've seen the *effect* of being surrounded by demands and pressures. It's stress. We've also touched on the *cause* of this stress, *e.g.*, high expectations, deadlines, fear for our safety and security: see *Chapter 6*. Now we need to investigate these causes further. We know what promotes feelings of worry and anxiety; those little voices in our heads- our S.T.O.P: Stupid Traumatising Overprotective Parent. It sits there drip-feeding us F.E.A.R or Future Events Aren't Reality. However, if we are really honest about this, we are the ones walking around feeding our S.T.O.P in the first place. We chose what we eat, read, listen to etc. This creates a negative feedback loop.

So if we are serious about being a Stress Ninja, then we need to monitor what we allow in to feed our S.T.O.P. We need to start paying attention to what we ingest. I'm not talking about food just yet, that's for later. I am actually talking about everything else we come into contact with. Most people walk around in a perpetual state of fear because the media is constantly informing us that all aspects of our lives, from our safety to our money, are under constant attack. Yet, it is US paying attention to these things.

However, the really damaging drivers are the more obscure, little things that chip away at us without our being aware of them. For example, I saw a client recently who had started experiencing anxiety for the first time in her life. This started at the same time as her last birthday. You're probably thinking the same as me, it's just anxiety related to her age right?

Well, after further investigation it transpired that one of her birthday presents had been an automatic, motion sensing air freshener. Some of these products have proven links with depression and anxiety. Whether that was the case here we'll never know, but the solid fact is that as soon as she removed it from her environment, her anxiety went with it. We had identified and removed the stress cause.

Doing a 'root cause analysis' doesn't take a lot of effort, but it does take a bit of bravery. Realising that we are surrounded by things in our environment that effectively have control over us is one thing, but understanding that we actually have ultimate control over them is a scroll of empowerment .

So, if we want to permanently reduce our stress and not just paper over the cracks, we need to understand the power of GIGO and QIQO.

> There is no more clear an example of papering over the cracks of stress than going to a doctor and being prescribed antidepressants!

GIGO and QIQO

What's GIGO? No, it's not a camp pop star. It's actually an age old computer term, it stands for 'Garbage In Garbage Out.' It means that the quality of the results obtained from a computer is only as good as the quality of the data that's fed into it in the first place. We can also apply this to us humans.

So GIGO boils down to a simple question:

Are you prepared to tune in and notice the things that are having a negative influence on you, then actively filter out and eradicate these things from your life?

If you are then this is the key to true stress management. The road to being a Stress Ninja.

GIGO applies to everything. The important thing here is that we need to start noticing what we are allowing into our system. I'm talking about everyone and everything we allow ourselves to come into contact with, because everything affects us. But we have a choice. We can adopt QIQO instead. What's that? Simple, it's the opposite of GIGO: Quality In Quality Out, and if we want to be a Stress Ninja we had better start adopting it as our strategy going forward!

Possessions

GIGO: If we have a constant feeling of being overwhelmed and out of control, then we need to examine our environment. The more things we own the more our energy is dissipated. The happiest and most organised people I know are usually minimalists, neat and tidy, with few possessions. The people who just can't seem to get it together are usually untidy and, well, just own lots of 'stuff.' Even stuff we can't see has an effect on us, think about your loft or your garage or even your desk at work. Is it untidy? Is that a nice feeling?

Does mess fill you with dread? Maybe it doesn't. Maybe being surrounded by stuff just doesn't bother you. Well, what about the simple mechanics of the situation; the more stuff you have the easier it is to misplace things. I don't know about you but searching for essential, mislaid items sends my stress gauge pretty high very quickly.

 Mess equals stress!

QIQO: Think about an area in your life that is full of junk, a wasted unusable space. Now think about hiring a skip and dumping the lot. Imagine cleaning, dusting and redecorating that area and leaving it clean and tidy. Isn't that a better feeling associated with an area in your life? I don't know about you, but getting rid of stuff is a wonderful, almost spiritual feeling.

As you know I like to include real world examples. I had a client who had just landed a senior role in a large company in London. She felt she'd been lucky getting the job, but keeping it would be a miracle. That probably wasn't true, but as I've told you before, perception is everything. Her feeling that way could have sabotaged the job.

She was shocked when I knew she was a hoarder. I worked out a program where she dumped, gave away or sold most of her possessions. The transformation was stunning. She just oozed competence and confidence. This is not the only case of this kind. See, it's very hard to be untidy when we have lots of space and few possessions. If our safety zone, our domain, our space, is clean, tidy and organised then so we will be.

Clothes

OK, so we've got rid of all of our junk. Now we can start on our wardrobe. Simple rule, if you haven't worn it in the last 12 months get rid of it.

GIGO: Don't wear something because it looked great when you bought it. Maybe it doesn't anymore. Got something that you like to just throw on because it's comfortable? That's great but just because it feels good doesn't mean you look good, and you certainly don't have to wear it in public. This stuff matters. Get noticed for the right reasons not the wrong ones. If I'm out shopping in a busy supermarket, no matter how busy or preoccupied

I am, I always tend to notice that person shopping in their pyjamas. It never fills me with admiration.

QIQO: Now we've cleared some space in our wardrobe, go out and get some more clothes. However, we should ONLY buy clothes that make us look good, that accentuate our physique. We need to do our research. There are loads of tips and tricks out there. For example one of my many nick names is 'No Neck' because my neck is 18 inches, therefore everything I wear has to be a V neck to make my 'headstump' look longer. We know when we look good, because we feel good. When we feel good our posture changes, we can't feel confident and stressed at the same time. One of my main weaknesses is suits. My dad had many Savile Row fully bespoke suits, and he told me at a young age:

'Life can be pretty tough, but if you look good then that's half the battle. People take you seriously. It amazes me that most people just don't get it.' – Alan Rollison

Stimulus

I'm talking here about things we use in order to stimulate or educate ourselves.

GIGO: The only time I read a news paper or watch the news is if I've been asked to be part of a quiz team, and then it's only the week before.

Let me tell you, I can feel a difference and it's not good. One of my friends is an absolute news junkie and is always shocked at my apathetic attitude towards current affairs.

> 'Karl, you should pay more attention to what's happening in the world!'
> 'Why? So I can walk around in perpetual fear, like you?'

You know what I call the news? **Organised Gossip.**

Know what I call Social Media? **Disorganised Gossip.**

I want to throw an idea out there: what if the media was a component of the same machine as the pharmaceutical companies? One keeps us scared and stressed by telling us that our health, finance, safety and future are under threat, and the other one puts its arm around us, opens up its coat full of antidepressants and growls 'don't worry I can sell you a solution.'

QIQO: We expand spiritually if we are educating ourselves. We live in the most amazing time in the history of mankind. It's only in the last few years that we have had instant access to the sum total of mankind's knowledge and endeavours via our phones and tablets. We can read the classics, learn about wars and conflicts and check out the latest scientific advancements. We have unlimited access to documentaries and classic films. The key to using all this information in a positive, enriching manner is to tune into our intuition and just ask ourselves 'is this benefiting me?'

We know when something is moving us forward or holding us back. It's a shame that with unlimited potential for education, people chose to read low standard publications and fill their heads with irrelevant news about irrelevant celebrities.

Music

I'm not just talking about actual music, but anything we actively chose to spend time listening to, *e.g.*, audio books, podcast, recorded debates etc.

GIGO: This isn't a lecture on what to listen to, but we need to be aware of how things affect us. I doubt if many of us have classical music on our playlist for the gym, but I'm almost certain we wouldn't listen to Thrash Metal to unwind at night, apart from anything else, it's rubbish. Again, this is obvious, but sometimes we can listen to stuff that evokes negative memories that can raise the needle on our Stress Meters without our noticing it.

QIQO: I love audio books, especially factual stuff. It's one of the things I love about technology, I can learn whilst running, driving, working, even swimming. Most people are amazed at what a different experience it is listening to a favourite book or film in audio format. There is no substitute for our own, unique imagination. This is why we love to be told stories.

One of my clients had trouble getting off to sleep, I recommended listening to relaxation and meditation in bed. This helped to some extent. She informed me that it was nowhere near as good as when her mum used to read to her from her favourite story book. So we arranged for her mum to record herself reading the entire book. The results were pretty incredible. Not only did it work a treat, but my client tearfully informed me that one day her mum won't be around anymore, but she'll always have the recording.

People

GIGO: This is simple but very important. Everyone we interact with has an effect on us, whether we are aware of it or not. The problem is, sometimes we put up with people out of habit. This is especially true of family. I've spoken to loads of people who have experienced constant and sustained bullying from relatives, even as adults. It always makes me laugh when I hear the old meaningless 'blood is thicker than water' rubbish. I mean, what has water got to do with anything? Anyway, it doesn't matter if it's our best friend, our parents, our partner or even our identical twin...

If a person is generating negative emotions within us via their views, opinions, aggression and assertiveness, or simply just by their energy, then we need to take appropriate action because it's NOT OK! We have enough negatives around us anyway, so the people we share our lives with should be part of the solution not the problem.

QIQO: We all know people that have a positive effect on us don't we? We walk into a social situation and they are there, and straight away we know we're going to have a good time. There is someone who, no matter what the situation, just a quick chat with them makes us feel better. Well we need to open our radars to people like this and seek them out. I have surrounded myself with amazing people. All of my friends are like minded; kind, generous, accepting and caring.

Thoughts

GIGO: This is what it's all about really. Thoughts don't actually exist in a physical, tangible sense yet they control everything we do. However, we are the ones in control of our own thinking. I had a client that dragged a massive weight of anger around with her everywhere she went - anger towards a long-dead, close relative. It affected everything in her life, her job, her relationships, but most important, her health.

'Let me summarise', I said *'you are allowing every aspect of your life to be destroyed by a collection of thoughts that don't actually exist, regarding a person that no longer exists.'* I got her to imagine the relative in the room begging for her forgiveness. It was very tearful, but it worked. Sometimes, it's not just a case of wilfully changing a negative thought, we have to get creative.

We need to start monitoring our thought processes and stop the negative ones, we're in control. Imagine your thoughts as objects on a conveyor belt. You are in charge of quality control, see yourself standing there with your clipboard watching the objects go by. When you spot a negative one, you can simply pick it up and throw it away.

QIQO: Ever sat down and had some negative thoughts about someone or something that's been really affecting you, then you suddenly changed your mind?

'Actually it's not that bad'

'I don't know what I'm worrying about'

'Wow, actually I think I could do it after all'

'Maybe they're not as bad as I thought, let's give them another chance.'

Isn't it a fantastic feeling? You know why it's a great feeling? Because you are taking responsibility for your thoughts and choosing to change them in a way that benefits you and others.

Accept the fact that we control our thoughts. We can remove the negative but it's easier still not to feed ourselves with negativity in the first place. When we feed ourselves with, and expose ourselves to, quality, there is only one possible outcome, QUALITY. Quality is a positive. We are growing. When we grow we get stronger and become more resilient to negatives.

So this chapter has been about what we choose to expose ourselves to *externally*, quality or garbage. The next chapter looks at choosing what we expose ourselves to *internally*.

One last thing, this isn't a sermon, I'm not preaching and this book isn't a prescription. I'm just trying to deliver the facts. Stress is bad for us, and the ultimate state as humans is happiness, and we just can't achieve it indulging in excessive GIGO!

16.   SUGAR EQUALS STRESS

He was about 3 stone overweight. He thought it was more like 3 pounds. He had greasy hair and bad skin. 'So, is your wife overweight too?'He was taken aback by the question.

'You must be joking! She is the fittest person I've ever met. She teaches yoga, runs in her spare time and only eats yoghurt, fruit, honey, nuts, berries and fish, and mainly drinks water. She doesn't eat processed food or sugar and, even if we go out, she'll only have one glass of wine.'

'Why does that annoy you so much?' He was surprised I'd noticed.

'Because she is always putting restrictions on herself, she is always monitoring what she eats. She needs to relax more.'

'So she suffers with stress then?'

He laughed. 'No not at all. She is the most relaxed person I know. In fact the only time she gets angry is when she catches me eating cakes, chocolate or sweets.'

'So you don't restrict what you eat at all?'

'No, why would I? No one tells me what to do. I eat cakes, chocolate, drink sweet coffee, energy drinks, vodka and coke, wine, whatever I want, when I want; and I'm way too busy to exercise,' he proudly exclaimed.

'So let me just get this straight. Your wife controls what she eats, doesn't ingest sugar, or processed food and ensures she is always hydrated, she's always exercising and never gets stressed.'

'That's about the sum of it yeah.'

'So remind me why you are here?'

'Because I don't have a stressful job and I have a great marriage, but I never seem to have any energy and I'm always feeling anxious.'

We can't go through life doing whatever we want and be happy, it just doesn't work that way.

> *Whatever the addiction is, you'll rarely meet a genuinely happy addict.*
>
> *– Karl Rollison*

Discipline and moderation are key. This is PARTICULARLY important when we refer to sugar...

What would happen if too much water went into the river Thames? London would flood causing catastrophic damage to one of the best cities in the world. *Banks and financial institutions would flood, but on the downside, people would die.* The results would be felt around the world. However, luckily, London has the beautiful Thames barrier. The barriers go up and hold back the excess flow of the river.

We have a safety barrier too. It's in our brains, but rather than water the barrier gets activated if it detects excess sugar flow. If we didn't have this safety device, with the amount of sugar we consume these days, everyone would be slipping in and out of comas...and no, I'm NOT exaggerating.

However, the problem is that when the barriers are up, the supply of fuel to our brain is restricted. Our bodies then think we are starving so we consume more food. The chaos continues. Our poor brain then has to work out what to do with this stock pile of disgusting sweetness. It has a couple of choices: get rid of it, or modify it and keep it in case we need it later.

What happens if we binge on fizzy drinks, chocolate and sweets? We feel nauseous. This is the first warning that we may need to purge our system. If we keep eating we *will* vomit and it WON'T be pleasant. I remember puking up as a kid due to eating a whole Easter egg. It was *weeks* before I could face chocolate again! The other thing that happens is the brain has to do complex calculations of how much insulin to produce in order to get this sugar out of our blood and safely stored as fat.

This is another thing. The mechanism for stockpiling fat was developed a long time ago, at a time when we had no option but to go out and hunt. Hunting takes a lot of energy so we needed a reserve just in case we were unsuccessful. We still use this same system, but the problem is, now food is readily available everywhere, and we don't have to use any energy to acquire more, so we just add to our already plentiful reserves.

You've now seen throughout this book, our brain's NUMBER ONE job is to protect us. Not only is it constantly monitoring the environment for potential external attacks, but when we eat sugar it tries to keep us safe internally. The poor thing, is it any wonder that we are so stressed?

The truth is we are eating more sugar than at any time in history! Our consumption of it has been skyrocketing year on year for the last three hundred years and we haven't had time to evolve to deal with it. The problem is 'added sugar'. This is stuff added to processed food and drink, not the natural sugars found in fruit and milk etc. Some studies suggest that added sugar consumption has doubled in the last 50 years. Separate UK and US medical research show that Parkinson's, Alzheimer's, diabetes and obesity have also doubled in the last 50 years. Do you see a pattern here? If the end result of adverse sugar consumption is severe, life threatening health issues doesn't it follow that we will be experiencing massive amounts of stress on the way?

> *It's no coincidence that STRESSED is DESSERTS spelt backwards.*
>
> *– Anonymous (I wish I'd thought of it).*

When we stress we produce Cortisol and Adrenalin. These hormones have a direct effect on our Melatonin production, this affects our sleep. We need sleep in order to grow (remember there are two states of existence, if we aren't growing we are shrinking) and this is the time when our brains do essential housekeeping, including cell replacement. Like any building work, we need the right materials. It's been proven that when we are tired we crave sugar so we eat rubbish processed food containing sugar.

Did you know that the vast majority of obese people are actually suffering from malnutrition? That's right, these people are stuffing their faces all day long but they are actually starving! There is a large amount of stuff going in, but it is not the stuff the body needs. These people are usually unconsciously aware of this. That is why they need to keep eating, because their brains are waiting for the good stuff. *I wonder if they fill their cars up with lemonade instead of petrol, hoping that the car doesn't notice.*

The brain is in emergency mode so they eat more food to try and stop the cravings, but THIS DOESNT WORK. So they get fat and then hate their appearance so they comfort eat junk food. In an attempt to control this, they consume diet foods containing sinister things like Aspartame, which was banned by the FDA in America TWICE because it's a toxin and has potential links to brain tumours.

The ironic thing is that saturated fat is actually good for us, we have been eating it since we were cavemen, but fat has been replaced with low fat diet food and drinks containing Trans-fatty Acids, which again are toxins. So not only are we fighting these toxins but the low fat food contains sugar. That's why eating this stuff doesn't satisfy us and actually makes us hungrier, perpetuating this cycle!

WHAT'S THE ANSWER?

SO we all love sweetness. We NEED sugar for energy and to survive. Convenience food is anything but convenient. Diet food is toxic. Diet foods make us hungrier.

Well there IS an answer. There is something that can de-stress us, improve our sleep and, what's more, eating it will actually help us TO LOSE WEIGHT? Too good to be true? This is one time when I believe it IS TRUE. Read the next chapter for life changing information.

17.   ONCE UPON A TIME...

...there was a kingdom ruled by giants. These giants called themselves 'wise' yet they wandered the land in constant fear of things that would never happen. Their favourite food was sweet things and, being very clever, they developed a way to harness a natural substance that made them feel a bit better about being scared all the time. They liked this stuff so much they kept eating more and more until, eventually, they realised it was killing them and making them fat. So they made another not-so-natural substance and, in a panic, put that in everything, to make them thin. The problem was that this stuff killed them as well. In this land lived other creatures. The wise ones called all other creatures 'dumb animals' perhaps because they didn't kill each other for money. There was one creature in particular that had lived on the land for a hundred million years before the giants. It was a tiny, beautiful, fury hardworking little fellow that possessed amazing magical qualities. It lived in a large home with a big family and its magic was so powerful that when its mummy got too old to produce babies it could make a magic potion, feed it to a normal baby and turn it into another

mummy, and not even the wisest of the wise could work out how it did it. So they chose to ignore it instead.

One of the other magical potions these creatures produced was identical in taste to the sweetness the giants craved so much. Not only was this potion delicious to the giants but it could solve most of the problems that the giants had. The problem was that the rulers of the land were extremely stupid and greedy and refused to accept the fact that the little furry creatures could produce something far greater than they ever could. This is called arrogance and this, along with greed, led to the death of the giants and the furry ones flourished.

OK, I made up the last bit but it's always made me laugh that Homo Sapiens means 'wise man.' I mean, *we weren't given that title you know?* We GAVE ourselves that! The arrogance of man will always be his downfall.

Anyway, it doesn't take a genius to realise that that little story above is about man and the little creatures in question are honey bees. The magic potion that turns normal bees into Queens is Royal Jelly and the other magic potion is Honey. I didn't want to write a book that involved nutrition, but I think Honey is SO important that I've dedicated a whole chapter to it. I would love to write a book about it but it's already been done, it's called 'The Honey Diet' by Mike McInnes and I would highly recommend it.

Now, I've been promoting honey for many years and I've used it to replace sugar for a long time. There is a little busy coffee shop in Drury lane that once told me that I account for half the honey they go through in a week. I had a full medical around that time and my blood sugar levels were at the lower side of normal. You know I like to include as much empirical information as possible, so here are the benefits I've experienced myself, and heard from, friends, family and clients, but before I list them: DISCLAIMER TIME.

"If you are planning on changing your diet in any way it is your responsibility to consult your GP."

Get your blood level tested (or purchase an electronic glucose monitor) then weigh yourself each morning. Buy a heart rate monitor and take it a few times a day. Get a feel for the average reading on your stress gauge.

Then what you need to do is buy some good quality set honey. Don't bother with Manuka Honey, it's OK but it's ridiculously expensive and nothing beats the health benefits of locally sourced natural honey.

A full hour before bed dissolve a tablespoon of honey in hot water. Yes, that's not a typo I said TABLESPOON. Let it dissolve and drink it up.

In the morning, rather than a coffee, dissolve a teaspoonful of honey in hot water. You could put some lemon in with it too. This will kick-start your metabolism and also loads your liver up with glycogen. That's it. After a week or so you will start to notice the difference. You will start to notice an increase in energy, focus and vitality. Go and check your blood levels again. Check your blood pressure and stress gauge readings again. Everything should have come down.

If this is taken seriously the results are amazing. Out of my friends, family and clients I have had reports of:

- High blood sugar levels dropping down to normal in a few weeks

- Borderline diabetics returning to normal in a short time

- Vastly improved sleep patterns

- Massively increased levels of concentration and focus

- Super levels of energy

- Clearer skin and eyes

- Lower blood pressure

- Increase memory

- Vastly reduced aches and pains

- AND, of course, *VASTLY* reduced levels of stress and anxiety!

I want to share something else with you that you might find hard to comprehend,

**This small adjustment will help you lose weight!**

Too good to be true? This stuff has absolute magical properties.

Read on…

Honey:

- Is the ONLY food stuff that doesn't spoil. Archaeologists have found pots full of honey in Egyptian tombs that dated back over 3000 years, and it was still perfectly *EDIBLE*!

- *Is an antioxidant*, effectively reducing cell damage.

- *Is antibacterial*, Honey is used by vets and doctors in hospital to treat wounds

- Can *reduce* blood pressure.

- *Is anti-inflammatory*, reducing inflammation and swelling, therefore pain.

- *Contains antimicrobial properties,* kills microorganisms but doesn't harm us.

- *Can be an antihistamine*, especially local Honey. Great for Hay fever, etc.

In the previous chapter I talked about how excess sugar attacks the brain, but we have a safety barrier. The problem is, with the barriers up, we can't get fuel and we think we are starving so we crave more high sugar food. OUR BRAINS ARE CONSTANTLY STRESSED. **Honey doesn't trigger the barrier.**

The truth is:

We have NEVER in the history of mankind eaten as much sugar as we do now. We have only been eating refined sugar for the past 300 Years. Our bodies don't know how to deal with it. However, we have been eating honey since BEFORE we were human. Our bodies know exactly how to metabolise it! It's like a hug from an old friend. It de-stresses our bodies and our livers, but most of all, our brains!

This means that when we are asleep our brains don't have to stress about how much insulin to produce to store the excess sugar as fat because it knows what to do with honey. It can breathe a sigh of relief. It knows how to use honey and has all the materials to replace cells so we start operating effectively.

I'm not telling you to change your diet. I'm just giving you the facts. Knowledge is Power! However, remember, if you're stressed all the time it's probably because of the GIGO principle, Garbage In equals Garbage Out. If you want to expose yourself to Quality from your environment AND internally the ONLY result you will get out will be QUALITY. Honey is high in calories but then again in wouldn't be much of an energy food if it wasn't. A quality life has no room for stress! QIQO

Last word: Just because honey is good for us and tastes great it doesn't mean we can eat loads of it! Remember what I said in **Chapter 3**, even water is toxic if we consume too much!

There is something else about eating honey that I can personally vouch for, if you include a big dollop in a glass of hot water first thing in the morning it loads up your liver with glycogen, and you don't get a craving for food at all until the late afternoon. I sometimes add honey to high altitude coffee, coconut oil and grass fed butter as well. Butter in coffee? It's gorgeous and gives you great focus and energy. This is my version of Bulletproof coffee, check it out for yourselves.

We can't argue with results. Try the honey diet for a few weeks and see how you feel. It's not chemicals or medication but natural. What have you got to lose?

Stress Ninja says...

"I bet you are feeling empowered right? This stuff IS obvious but the best things in life are. You are well on your way now...!"

18.   ASK THE EXPERT

In the previous chapters we looked at the things we allow ourselves to be exposed to. Sometimes it can be difficult to decide if something is holding us back or moving us forward. Wouldn't it be great if there was someone we could ask? An expert we could consult? Well there is. There is an absolute authority who knows absolutely everything about us, our desires, hopes and fears. Who is it? Well, it's us!

Only we have experienced everything we have, and only we truly know how we feel. The key thing is tuning into the unconscious mind. Sometimes it's difficult to hear it, so we can ask it direct questions. As a Hypnotherapist I use this system of speaking directly to the unconscious mind all the time. I ask it a question and ask for the response to be non verbal, but a muscle movement instead. It's called Ideomotor Response or IMR. 'Ideo' means idea and 'motor' means muscle movement so it literally means how a thought, usually prompted by a question, will evoke a certain, unconscious muscle response. We are basically bypassing the conscious mind.

What's really cool about IMR is that we can use it on ourselves at any time whilst we are awake. This really comes into its own when applied to decision making. Remember what we said in chapter two about human cells in a Petri dish? Cells will move towards nutrients and away from toxins. Well, guess what? WE are comprised of about 70 trillion of those cells and we have the same unconscious response to our environment, we naturally move away from danger and towards nourishment.

Imagine standing in front of a table, feeling hungry and there is a plate with a metal room-service type cover. We don't know what's under the cover but we are asked to remain as still as possible. The cover is removed revealing a sea of writhing maggots. We would move backwards, even if we tried not to. What about if the cover contained lovely, fresh, warm cakes. Chances are we would move forwards. These movements would be outside of our awareness.

This would be an example of our unconscious mind trying to either protect or nourish us. This same system can be tapped into and used as a very powerful Stress Ninja tool.

IMR - The Leaning Test

OK, so find somewhere quiet, were you feel safe and comfortable.

You'll need to be nice and relaxed. Do any technique in this book that you feel appropriate or perhaps the OnePoint technique.

The floor needs to be flat and even. First off you need to get a feel for the technique.

Take your shoes off and stand with your feet shoulder width apart and allow your arms to hang by your sides.

Now think of something you love. A person, a food, a place...try and get a clear image of it and say 'yes yes yes yes.'

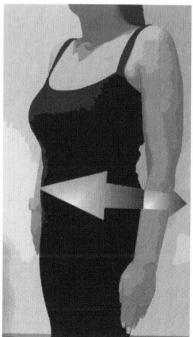

Notice you are starting to lean forwards?

Now walk around the room and take some deep breathes (this acts as a reset).

Stand as you were before, but this time think of something you hate, something repulsive, a food, a place, Tony Blair, anything. This time say 'no no no no.'

Notice how you start to lean back?

Now you know how the technique feels. Walk around the room taking nice relaxing deep breaths and think about something that may have come up in the previous chapter. Think about something you're not sure about. Someone or something that you feel may be GIGO.

A decision you need help with. Say out loud, for example, 'is this person good for me?' It needs to be a clear question that requires a distinct yes or no answer.

Sometimes the answers take a bit of bravery to acknowledge.

Don't underestimate the power of this technique. There are some powerful people around the world making important decisions every day using this method.

Ok, so this is a great technique for assisting with decision making, but it's not that practical for when you're out and about, so there is a simplified version that you can do anywhere.

IMR -The nail rub.

Gently place you're middle finger on top of your index finger and softly rub the nail backwards and forwards, notice how it feels.

Now think of walking on a beautiful day, feeling amazing and breathing beautiful fresh air, say 'yes yes yes yes.' The nail should feel nice and smooth.

Think now of walking a muddy field, on a cold, wet and windy day with a severe hangover and itchy clothes, say 'no no no no.' You should feel the nail get sticky or rough, it should feel different in some way.

Now pick something from the previous chapter that you need help with. This is really good checking for food intolerances. Pick up something in one hand and rub your nail with the other hand. IMR will let you know if you should eat it or not.

You can also do this test by rubbing the thumb and index fingers together. I helped someone discover a lifelong food intolerance using this technique. That's quite impressive when you consider doctors and allergy consultants failed to find it. We are our own experts we just need to know what questions to ask then listen out for the answers.

The thing is, I'll keep saying this, our bodies are communicating with us all the time. Why wouldn't they be? Our brains and our bodies are not separate modules, we are one complete unit. IMR is a very powerful system for tuning into our intuition and hearing the subtle guidance of our unconscious mind.

Our aim in life should be to achieve harmony or homeostasis. In order to do this effectively we need to get the basics right, *e.g.*, hydration and rest. If we are thirsty we don't ignore that feeling do we? We have a drink, yet it amazes me that people try to ignore that overwhelming urge for rest. If we are serious about self protection and stress defence, we need to make sure we are getting enough sleep. I will cover this in the next chapter.

19.   SLEEP

I've already told you that stress is at the highest levels in the history of our species. Did you also know that we are now sleeping less than at any time in history? Also type two diabetes, obesity, Parkinson's disease and Alzheimer's are at record highs and increasing. That's no coincidence. All these things are directly related to each other. On average we are now sleeping two hours less than we did 50 years ago and I believe it is getting worse by the day. I've been conducting my own survey on sleep for years. I ask every client I see about their sleeping habits regardless of their issue. The results are shocking. Around 80 percent of the people I speak to have sleeping problems. Some fall asleep OK but are wide awake a few hours later and others sleep through the night but have trouble falling asleep in the first place.   What shocks me more though is the general attitude of indifference to this problem, 'I'm used to it', 'It runs in my family', 'I can catch up at the weekends.' The worst thing I hear are boasts about how little sleep is needed by someone. Listen, sleep isn't a joke, it isn't something that once served a purpose but we no longer needed. In fact, it's the exact opposite. With our modern diet and lifestyle sleep is now more relevant than ever. A clear and terrifying example of this is the fact that road traffic accidents due to tiredness are now the highest they've ever been in history. *I wish people would take sleep more seriously.*

A few years ago I was coaching an entrepreneur in Dubai who was apparently worth in the region of £50 million.

'You are an extremely successful businessman but you collapse into bed at about 12 then you drag yourself out of it again at around 4 am? So what is it I can help you with?', I asked.

'I just feel anxious, stressed and tired all the time.'

'But you're only sleeping 4 hours a night!'

'That's right,' he beamed. 'I only need 4 hours.'

'But you just told me that you're stressed, anxious and tired all the time. Do you think there is a distinct possibility that perhaps you actually need more than 4 hours sleep?'

'Na, I've always had 4 hours. A lot of people call me the "Machine" because of how hard I work without rest. Everyone I work with is in awe of my abilities.'

'You don't actually need to work and could lie in bed and spend the day relaxing and playing Golf, but instead you choose to work extra hard, mainly to impress people with your prowess, but this regime is actually affecting your health.'

'I don't care. I'm not going to change my sleeping pattern, I'm too busy. There must be other things I can do to deal with the tiredness.'

'You are a highly regarded and well respected, rich, successful powerful business man.'

He slowly nodded with a sly grin, he obviously hears this sort of thing a lot.

'However, for the record, I don't think you're a machine...I think you're an idiot!'

That wiped the smile of his face.

Let me ask a question: How much water do you think we need to drink every day? If you think its 8 glasses then think again. The '8 glasses' thing is nonsense, made up on the spur of the moment many years ago and pushed forward by (surprise surprise) all the major bottled water companies. We have a very efficient mechanism that tells us exactly when and how much water to drink, it's called thirst and it's been keeping us alive for quite a while. What's my point here? Well we have another million year old mechanism that lets us know when it's time for rest, relaxation and sleep...It's called *'feeling tired.'* If you ignore it for long enough something, be it mental or physical, WILL snap! Ensuring we get adequate rest is the very basics of self protection. The essence of the Stress Ninja.

The fact is, when we have finished our days work our systems housekeeping begins. This is the period where our brains and bodies do essential maintenance, replacing cells, digesting food, sorting through and filing away relevant thoughts and memories. However, sleep isn't just a lump of 'stuff', it's a highly complex series of brain frequency variations. The REALLY important maintenance only occurs during part of the cycle. So, no matter how much sleep you think you need, if you're tired all the time, chances are you need more. Probably 7 – 9 hours like the rest of us.

Margaret Thatcher only needed 4 hours sleep but people like that are few and far between. These people have something called SSS or 'Short Sleeper Syndrome' and they make up less than 1% of the world population. This, however, isn't a superpower but a medically recognised sleep disorder.

Let me say something else quite terrifying, when we are sleep deprived our bodies go into a sort of panicked survival mode and we start to extract a vastly increased amount of calories from the same amount of food. So even though we are exhausted our fuel system has stepped up its efficiency. This was very useful when we were cavemen and had to be awake to find more food, but not great now. In short when we are tired we are actually gaining weight. Prolonged tiredness leads straight to obesity.

This is all scary stuff right? Don't worry, all we need is a...

Sleep plan

I've successfully helped numerous people over the years with sleep related issues. I have given people a selection or combination of the following recommendations. Experiment, and do some or all of the following. They are all perfectly safe and completely natural alternatives to sinister, damaging and addictive sleeping tablets.

This process of adjusting our habits and practises with the view to increasing the quantity and quality of our sleep is known as **Sleep Hygiene**.

- *Make your bedroom a sleep zone. Remove ALL technology from the room, including the TV, tablets and phone. Charge all of your devices in another room where you can't hear the things ping and vibrate. The exception here being if you listen to sleep assistance, relaxation or meditation audio, in this instance put the device out of sight and in flight mode.*

- *Remove all clutter and have as little furniture and 'stuff' as possible.*

- *Redecorate your room in a nice, warm, soft, relaxing colour like eggshell blue.*

- *Buy the best bed sheets you can afford, perhaps Egyptian cotton.*

- *Turn the alarm clock away. You've set the alarm. It will tell us when to wake up. You don't need to keep staring at it. That just makes us more aware of having a time limit.*

- *Sleep with the windows open. Fresh air aids restful sleep, but you also need the bedroom to be the coolest room in the house, between 17 and 19 degrees. Turn the heating off in this room. Heat and sleep don't mix. Ever slept well in a heat wave?*

- *Have good old fashioned, interesting books by your bed. Read before sleep.*

- *When it gets dark at night, switch off the blue lights on your devices and make them a softer colour. Most devices have a night shift mode to aid sleep.*

- *Don't use any technology or social media an hour before bed, don't worry you won't miss anything.*

- *Don't drink caffeine after midday and try to exercise at some point in the day.*

- *Make sure you are fully hydrated. Every aspect of night-time housekeeping requires water.*

- *Have a hot shower or bath an hour before bed. Our bodies naturally cool down when we sleep so this enhances that effect and makes us drowsy.*

- *Try to avoid alcohol although some research suggests a small glass of red wine can aid sleep.*

- *Spray your room and pillow with natural lavender oil, proven to aid sleep.*

- *If you do nap in the day do not exceed 20 minutes. This is the ideal period of time to refresh, any longer can affect night time sleep.*

- *As you've seen, Honey aids sleep and de-stresses the brain, so have a heaped teaspoon in hot water half hour before bed.*

- *With your honey eat a couple of Kiwi fruits. There have been many trials that support the theory that kiwi fruit aids sleep, and I find they work pretty well.*

- *Try allowing a natural Rescue Remedy melt to dissolve on your tongue at night.*

- *Spend some time before bed in silence. Just focus on your breathing. This is mindfulness. Or, once in bed, do the technique in* **Chapter Ten**, *lowering your frequency.*

- *Prebiotics. New research shows that dietary prebiotics increase NREM sleep. This is the Non Rapid Eye Movement stage of our sleep cycle, the stage where all of the repair work is done and growth hormones are released. So when we take prebiotics we are actually improving the efficiency and quality of our overall system, making ourselves highly resistant to stress. You could take a daily prebiotic supplement or, alternatively, you could get everything you need from your diet. Prebiotics are found in: bananas, leeks, lentils, beans, garlic, onions and artichokes.*

- *The circadian rhythm. In* **Chapter Nine** *we learnt about the ultradian rhythm, these are brain frequency cycles that affect our focus and attention every 90 minutes or so throughout the day. There is a bigger 24 hour rhythm that controls our life, called circadian rhythm. This is basically our body clocks telling us when it's time for bed and when it's time to wake up. We have many clocks in our bodies - our brain, our hearts, our liver and a variety of other organs. If these get out of sync with each other it upsets our sleep and causes massive stress and* *anxiety. The best way to get these systems synchronised and promote homeostasis is by getting as much natural light as possible. I think that's why we feel tired when we spend long periods of time outside, and not really 'all that fresh air' as our parents used to tell us.*

Here's another technique you can use by itself or in conjunction with some or all of the above.

 Sleep aid. 4-7-8 breathing

Get comfortable in a quiet place and position your tongue on the roof of your mouth behind your teeth.

1. Breathe in deeply through your nose for the count of 4

2. Pause for the count of 7

3. Breathe out for the count of 8 making an 'ahhh' noise as you do this, be aware of your muscles relaxing.

4. Go back to number 1. Keep doing this for as long as possible.

You will, at some point feel a comfortable shift in your energy and anxiety levels

Being hydrated and well rested is one of the best natural feelings we can experience and it's a great foundation for managing stress. Need more proof? What's the opposite of this? What is one of the worst feelings we can experience? Hangovers. These are a result of not having quality rest and extreme dehydration. In this situation we are never far away from anxiety and panic attacks, so we have basically placed ourselves in a volatile situation where we have massively raised our susceptibility to acute stress.

If you are really serious about being a Stress Ninja then you really need to take your sleep seriously. As you've seen, stress is and always will be part of our lives. You now have the weapons and mindset needed to defend yourself against all forms of attack.

So with a good rest we cultivate a positive mindset, a feeling of positive resilience against negatives. To give it it's technical name, *confidence*.

Stress Ninja says...

"Isn't it incredible to know just how amazingly versatile and resilient you are as a human? You already have all the answers!"

20. CONFIDENCE

If you have followed everything in this book, read all the Scrolls and practiced all of the Stars, and you are well rested and hydrated, you should start to experience something. This thing is warm, comfortable and quite possibly one of the nicest feelings we can experience. It's called...

Confidence

When was the last time you felt really confident about something? Think back now; try to remember all of the details. Perhaps it was at a party, at work, in a social gathering, on holiday. Were you stressed? No of course you weren't.

When we feel confident we produce Oxytocin, the Love hormone. Remember there is a very distinct relationship between Oxytocin and the Stress Hormone Cortisol. As one goes up the other one comes down.

Posture power

I love watching people's body language, it fascinates me. You don't need to be an expert to tell when someone is feeling confident or vulnerable. It's plain for everyone to see. We express it in our posture. I see the relationship between our physical bodies and our emotions like an electric motor. If you put electricity *in*, the motor turns. If you turn the motor manually you get electricity **out**. So with regards to our bodies, for example, if you are happy you smile right? It also follows that if you smile you start to feel happy.

 Smile. This is a very simple example of the above. Place a pencil between your teeth so that it touches both corners of your mouth. Now GENTLY push the pencil back and grip it in your back teeth. This forces a smile. After a while you will feel a positive shift in your mood. This is handy because it's something you could do at work. Some people find this uncomfortable, if we are feeling discomfort it equals stress so guess what? If any technique in this book feels in anyway unpleasant – don't do it. ☺

Our posture affects our mental state and our mental state affects our posture

Try this:

Negative Posture

Sit down and hang your head low.

Put your elbows on your knees.

Hunch your shoulders and look at the floor for 90 seconds.

Quietly say 'no, no, no, no, no.'

At some point you will feel a distinct negative shift in your state. It's not nice.

In this position try to have a happy thought. Hard isn't it?

Now walk around the room to reset your state of mind. Then try this:

Positive Posture Power

Stand up and place your feet shoulder width apart.

Take a deep breath in and place your fists on your hips like Superman.

Look up at the ceiling for 90 seconds.

Smile and breathe in.

When you breathe out say 'YES'

In this position try to think of something negative. I bet you can't.

There is a natural micro switch in our heads that switches moods according to the angle of our heads. We can tell when people are sad and dejected even if we don't know them, it's obvious. It's also easy to spot someone who exudes confidence. These are forms of energy exchanges, and remember, energy is contagious.

Milton Errickson was the best hypnotherapist that ever lived. He believed that the unconscious mind was always listening and willing to learn. He would use a whole range of techniques to help his clients, some obvious, some indirect, some conventional and others created by him, sometimes on the spot. As soon as he met his clients he would start the session, usually without them realising, and sometimes the session would continue long after they had departed.

For example, a client went to see him suffering from stress and anxiety. After the session he asked him to walk home from the office and count as many chimney pots as he could. Why did he do this? Well, in order to count chimneys he would have had to have looked up. When he looked up he would have opened his airways, but more importantly, he would have activated an alpha state in his brain and would have naturally adopted a confident posture. Apparently the client never needed another session.

So, guess what the next technique will be?

 Things are looking up

Take a note of your Stress Gauge number.

Go for a long walk.

See how many chimneys, TV aerials and aeroplanes you can count.

Check your Gauge after. Gone down hasn't it?

You want to know the really cool thing about the above technique? No one is going to look at you and think 'look at that weird person over there counting chimneys.' They are going to think 'That person looks pretty confident.'

However, the chances are no one will be looking at you at all, more about that in a bit.

We've seen that tipping our head down will activate negative feelings. As I mentioned in the introduction, stress is on the increase. This is due to the speed of life now, and the increase in demands placed on us. There is another reason...

Everyone is spending more and more time with their heads hung low. WHY? Because they are looking down at their phones! At their desks, in restaurants, on the train, in bed and now, the latest evolution; whilst walking. I call people who look down at their phones, oblivious to their surroundings, mobile zombies or **ZOMBILES**

If you want to be a true, confident Stress Ninja, not at the MERCY of your surroundings but the MASTER of them, then DONT BE A ZOMBILE!!

A Stark warning!

What happens in nature when there is an abundance of prey? The predators come out. It's feeding time. In the UK for a few days of the year the flying ants emerge, this causes chaos. Swallows and Swifts fill the skies and the formic acid in the ants turn greedy Seagulls into raging psychopaths. Well guess what? The same thing is happens in humanity. There is now an epidemic in the UK regarding Scooter, Moped and motor bike related crime. It's very easy for a bike passenger to violently attack and rob someone who has effectively relinquished awareness. Zombiles have no hearing, restricted eyesight. Their brains, hands and awareness are focused on their precious communication devices. They are mugger, rapist and murder fodder. It's going to get worse and will soon be a global pandemic. In the UK police won't even pursue two-wheeled criminals, they deem it too dangerous for all parties. If they do pursue, the clued-up baddies simply remove their helmets, this puts a definite stop to proceedings, the police don't want the little darlings to hurt their little headie-weadies.

I now need to deliver a serious fact that I want you to pay close attention to...

 *If you insist on walking around with your bag over your shoulder, your headphones on, listening to music whilst staring at your phone you WILL become a victim of crime, possibly violent. It's just a matter of time. Let me tell you this as well, when that happens you will have corrupted one of your basic human needs; your security. You think you are stressed now? Wait until you are too scared to leave the house! Answer this:*

! Do you really need to listen to music while you walk?

! Can that text message not wait?

! Is the middle of the street appropriate for engaging with Social Media?

! Is it safe to hold your phone in the air for that selfie?

 *Don't be a victim, be a Stress Ninja*

 The predator

This is actually more of a mission (should you decide to take it) than a technique. I do this with all of my students and some of my clients if relevant. I want you to imagine you are a dangerous, violent criminal. Like all professional baddies you are constantly on the hunt for job opportunities. Now as you walk around with a good posture and heightened awareness with your phone in your pocket and your eyes and ears open you'll need something to do. You could play 'I Spy' but it's not much fun by yourself. You could count chimneys. However, I want you to imagine you are on the hunt, you are on the lookout for prey to steal from. This is a great exercise because you will start to notice just how bad things are out there. You'll see just how many Zombiles are about, how stupid and unaware people have become. People have wilfully removed themselves from their environment. Make a note of how many people walk straight into you without even looking up from their phone, this has only started happening in the last few years...around the same time as the two-wheeled baddie explosion. After doing this for a while you will have the same reaction as most people, **'I can't believe I used to do that!'**

Start taking notice of other people, their attitude and demeanour and how this fits in with their posture. As a Stress Ninja you'll need to start doing your own research. If you meet someone who appears really confident, ask them about their stress levels. They may have some really good tips you could nick. If you think this is a bit weird, think again, I do this all the time and have done for years. If I see someone doing something that gets me curious, I'll ask them about it and I always have. I've never had a negative reaction yet. You know why? *Because people love talking about themselves.*

This leads me onto another reason to be confident. Most of the time most people don't actually notice us, but we go around in our little self conscious world thinking that everyone is looking at us. This is called...

THE SPOTLIGHT EFFECT: the phenomenon in which people tend to believe they are being noticed more than they really are. Seeing that we are constantly in the centre of our own world, we tend to overestimate how much other people notice us.

Think about it. Ever been in a situation where maybe you had a spot on your face, or your hair was a mess, or you had a stain on your shirt? To you, at the centre of your universe, it is the most prevalent and obvious thing on the planet. It dominates your whole world. You are so conscious of it you try a pre-emptive strike and actually point it out to someone. What do they say? 'Oh, to be honest, I never really noticed until you said.' So now you have drawn attention to something that would have gone unnoticed. In reality no one notices, even those that do only really care about their own spots, hair and stains. When I initially tell people about the spotlight effect they are usually a bit dejected at not being a prominent feature of everyone else's universe, after a while, though, most people find it liberating.

Don't take it personally

There is something else that I tell my clients when it comes to confidence. There's a guy called Don Miguel Ruiz, who wrote a book called the Four Agreements. I don't want to explore this in too much depth, but one of the agreements is 'Don't take anything personally.'

Whatever we are doing in the world from other people's perspective we are just part of the sea of humans. They may be the angry boss, the stroppy teenager, the rude shopkeeper or the arrogant waiter. They are all the centre of their own universes and we just briefly enter. So, remember, when someone jumps in front of you in a queue or cuts you up in a car, they probably don't know you and it usually isn't personal. It says more about them then it does about you. Because negative encounters with people can raise our stress levels and deplete our confidence, the really cool thing is, we are in charge of this. If we allow them to affect us then they are taking control over us, if we don't allow it to affect us then we are the ones in control.

Understand and accept

Can you now see that how you present yourself to the world matters? How something as simple as our posture can change the way the world sees us? Experiment with all of the techniques in this book and develop your own system. You'll be amazed how these things work. Realise that knowledge is power but the really powerful thing is not just understanding something but accepting it as life changing. Put faith in yourself this leads to THE most powerful thing on the planet...*SELF BELIEF!*

21.   BELIEF

If you've followed this book, read all the scrolls of enlightenment and practised the stars of empowerment then you should now have cultivated the MINDSET required for effective defence against any form of stress. You should now be in possession of all the WEAPONS needed to fight the enemy. You have everything you need to be a true Stress Ninja. There is just one thing missing. It's the glue that holds all of this together. What is it? It's belief! Belief is THE most powerful thing a human being can possess. How has any one in history achieved greatness, pushed boundaries, gone against popular opinion? Belief. Whether you put faith in god, your guardian angel, a trinket, one of the many holy books or yourself, it doesn't matter. What does matter is the outcome.

Believe that you can defend yourself against anything. Believe you don't have to listen to anyone or anything. Believe that you are your own expert and you will never let yourself down. Believe that you are not stuck and can do and be anything you want.

The Power of Belief

It was believed for about a thousand years that no human could ever run a mile in under 4 minutes. Athletes tried in vain throughout history trying to break this barrier. Doctors and other experts warned that, not only was this feat impossible, but extremely dangerous. Roger Bannister didn't care what anyone thought. He knew he could do it. On May 6th 1954 he broke the 4 minute mile. This became worldwide news. His achievement showed not only what was possible but, more important, the power of belief, because just 46 days later John Landy broke Bannister's record.

I mentioned earlier about the Placebo effect. This is a Latin word and it means 'I shall please.' This is the official definition:

A beneficial effect produced by a placebo drug or treatment which cannot be attributed to the properties of the placebo itself and must therefore be due to the patients belief in that treatment.

However, there is an opposite of this. It's called the Nocebo effect or 'I shall harm.' We are told from a young age by teachers, friends, the media and our family that we have limitations. This becomes our core programming throughout life and it is replayed throughout our lives by the little voices in our heads. Our S.T.O.P:

You can't leave your job

You'll never be able to do that, you're not clever enough

If you went there by yourself you could get attacked. Best to stay at home

You can't do that college course, remember what happened last time.

Etc, etc, etc, etc. ad nauseam...another Latin expression that means something is repeated so much that it becomes tiresome. Aren't you bored with hearing this stuff?

Knowledge is power. I don't know how long you've been awake reading this, but I bet your S.T.O.P has already fed you a negative already. Make a list, see how stupid they can be.

People don't think of limiting beliefs as the Nocebo effect, but I know that they absolutely are. These beliefs will hold you back, triggering panic and stress if we go against them. When you are held back you are in protection. When you are in protection you are not growing. You are producing the stress hormone Cortisol instead of the Love hormone Oxytocin. This suppresses your immune system allowing the opportunistic pathogens to run riot in your systems, affecting your health. What do you think?

Now I want to demonstrate the power of the Nocebo and Placebo effect. I show this same technique to my martial arts students and my clients. I want to demonstrate that YOU ARE THE ONE IN CHARGE!

 The Nocebo effect.

Sit down somewhere quiet and comfortable. You will really need to use your imagination for this one. First off, roll your sleeve up if you need to. I want you to expose your arm.

Imagine you have fallen asleep on a hot sunny day. You slept in the shade but you had inadvertently left your forearm in direct sunlight. I want you now to look down at your own forearm. See it being an angry, raw burnt reddish colour and swollen. You want to rub medicated cream on it but it's too painful to touch. You can feel it throbbing, it's so painful you're almost in tears.

Now take a deep breath in, pick a spot on your forearm, reach down with your other hand and pinch the skin hard and remember how much pressure you used.

On a scale of 0 to 10 how painful was the pinch? Remember the number

Now I want to shake your arms and walk around the room to do a reset.

Now, I want to show you the power of positive thinking. I want to show you the Placebo effect.

 The Placebo Effect

Sit back down again. This time I want you to imagine that you are a super hero that feels no pain. Your arm is tougher than steel and can smash through walls. It is super strong and impervious to all pain and damage. You can feel the power from it. Flex your arm, feel how powerful it is. Visualise your arm smashing through concrete as if it was a big stale cake.

Now reach down and pinch the same spot as before with the same pressure. What is the pain number now? How does it compare to the above?

This is a powerful demonstration of the power of visualisation to change a belief. Hopefully it demonstrates to you that we can change how we respond to a situation just by changing our thoughts. We are not at the mercy of our environments, but the master of them.

So if something is holding you back from doing something, then that something is usually YOU. This will cause you stress.

If there is something you want to move forward with, then it's your choice if you do or not. But if you don't, it will lead to stress.

Whatever IT is, IT is restricted and guided by your beliefs. Beliefs are just thoughts. We control our thoughts.

Using the power of visualisation I have helped people vastly increase their golf drive, bench press weight, punching power, jumping height and underwater swimming distances. I have helped people lose weight, gain muscle, run faster, run farther and decrease lap times. I even helped a little old lady smash boards with her hands. How? With the power of belief.

Here's another demonstration of this. Only do this if it is comfortable and you don't have a bad back.

 The Power of visualisation and belief

Stand with you feet shoulder width apart and raise your right arm in front of you. Now point your index finger. Look along the length of your arm and along to the tip of your finger.

Now slowly turn to the right looking down the length of your finger. Keep turning until you physically can't turn any further. Make a mental note on the wall of the distance you achieved. Try this again, keep going until you can't go any further. Again make a mental note. Don't move your feet and try it again, it'll probably be around the same point. This point represents your physical limit. This is a Nocebo.

Now we are about to generate a Placebo using visualisation and suggestion. Stay relaxed and keep standing in the same position. Take a deep breath, hold it and let it out until your lungs are completely empty. Breathe normally and close your eyes. With your eyes closed keep your arms by your side. I want you to imagine that your spine is now made of rubber. Your whole body is hyper flexible. With your eyes closed imagine holding your arm and finger out in front of you as before. Visualise looking along the length of your arm as before. Now start to turn. Imagine that you are slowly moving round and see your finger stop at the point you got to last time. Now see your arm continue past that point and on. Keep going right round. You are made of rubber. Keep going right round until you almost reach the front again having almost done a 360 degree turn.

Now open your eyes lift your arm and point your finger forward as before. Slowly turn around until you can't go any further.

I bet you are shocked at how much further you managed to go right? How cool is that? Using visualisation you can achieve anything. When you accept this fact you can change your beliefs!

I need to finish this chapter by telling you about one of my friends. I've known him for a long time and he has a very distinct, genuine characteristic that I haven't seen in many people...he doesn't experience stress like anyone I've ever met. I've been in numerous situations and adventures with him and I've watched him go through some pretty tough times. He has a very "can do" attitude and places himself in some pretty tough business and personal situations, and he just deals with them better than anyone I've met. One day I asked him for a formal interview regarding his strategy. This was his response.

'Whatever happens in my life I know I can deal with it. I am intelligent and resourceful and anything that happens I can resolve. I know this because I have successfully dealt with everything so far without dying. I just don't understand worrying about something that usually never happens anyway. I've never been in a life or death situation and, despite what the media would have us belief, I'm pretty sure I never will. But you know, if I did I'd either survive it or die. The most likely thing we'll encounter is natural death. Well, that's life. On a

day to day basis the most likely thing is financial challenges. Well, if I lost everything I'd start again, I'd build up my business. I did it before, it wasn't an accident. If I went bankrupt then so what? Lots of successful people have been bankrupt. If I lost absolutely everything then I am still a good person with good friends and family. I recon I've got a layer of about 30 people before I have to sleep in a cardboard box. The worst thing that could happen to me would be an illness. Well, I'd get better and if I didn't I'd die but I've got a will so what's to worry about?

The funny thing about this is that he actually isn't very intelligent or, come to think of it, very resourceful. But that is absolutely irrelevant because he **BELIEVES** he is, and the result of that is a fairly stress free life. A natural Stress Ninja.

With that in mind I want to set you some homework. I want you to compile a Bucket List. I want you to include everything you want to do in your life, no matter how small or how ridiculously big. It could include changing your hairstyle to climbing Mount Everest. It doesn't matter. It's YOUR list and no one else's business.

I wanted to make up a really relevant and thought provoking quote here but it's already been done.

Whether you think you can or you think you can't, you're probably right. – Henry Ford

I'd like to finish this chapter with a book recommendation. I get a lot of clients tell me that they feel stuck or in a rut. They believe they have no options in life, that they are in an impossible, catch 22 situation. Well do you have a few spare pounds and a few spare hours? There is a tiny book called 'Man's search for meaning' by Viktor Frankl. I bet you'll feel a WHOLE lot better about your predicament after reading it!

LAST WORD

So why did I ask you to do a bucket list? Because we need things to aim for in life. We need goals. We need a direction to head in, otherwise what's the point? Don't do what a lot of people do, they hate their jobs and their lives and live for the two weeks off they get every summer. Do you seriously think that we are the sum total of millions of years of evolution, to do that?!

The results of my findings are that people who stay doing something for other people without being true and honest to themselves, are the most stressed and unhappy people I've ever met. The ones that realise what they want to do with their lives are the ones that become Stress Ninjas.

Don't be a sheep in life. Don't trundle along feeling that your only sliver of happiness is your two weeks summer holiday. Do you feel stuck? Well, I'll let you in on a secret. You have a trillion trillion options! – Karl Rollison

---

Deathbed.

Right then, I've got something to tell you so you'd better sit down...you are dying! That's right, one day you'll be dead. We started dying as soon as we took our first breath. We only get allocated a finite amount of breathes, and you've already used loads of them up. So one day you WILL end up on your deathbed*.

*unless you get wiped out in a spectacular accident.

I want you to imagine you are on your deathbed. Look around your little hospital room. Hear the beeps of the machines you are attached to. Smell that hospital smell. Look down at your hands. There's a bit of paper with writing on it. It's your bucket list and none of the items are ticked off. How do you feel? All those dreams and aspirations that came to nothing. But don't worry because you worked really hard for someone else and you spent a lot of time worrying about things that never happened, so it wasn't a total waste.

If you're not already on your deathbed then it's not too late. So start ticking things off. Isn't it a great feeling when we've had a really productive day and got loads done? Well, just scale that up a bit. The key thing is to use visualisation for each thing. Don't just write them down but imagine you are doing them in vivid detail. This is giving your unconscious mind a clear instruction that this is something you desire.

Anyway, before I go. In case you doubt any of the stuff in this book, I want to tell you what the most common deathbed regrets are. You don't have to take my word for it, do your own research:

> *1. I wish I'd had the courage to live a life true to myself, not the life others expected of me.*
>
> *2. I wish I hadn't worked so hard.*
>
> *3. I wish that I had let myself be happier*

Let me tell you something else I know.

1. You'll never be ready, so you might as well do it anyway

2. You will make mistakes

3. Stop listening to your S.T.O.P, it will hold you back

4. Tune into your instincts, they will push you forward

5. You might make yourself look stupid on the way but...

6. **SO WHAT!?**

I want to leave you with my personal favourite mechanism for coping with the feelings of despair, anxiety or one of the worst situations a human can experience; feeling overwhelmed. It's sort of a combination of a scroll of enlightenment and a star of empowerment. It's a piece of knowledge that is really powerful and ties into the story of the Farmer and his horse in chapter

12. I didn't include it there because I wanted to leave it as the parting technique.

Imagine life is a maze. When you are experiencing problems you are on the ground level trying to find your way out. What if you could see the maze from the air? You would then be able to see exactly where you are, where you need to turn and which direction to head in. Well, you can't do that but you can choose to believe that maybe, just maybe, where you are is actually OK. <u>In the grander, bigger scheme of things, maybe you are exactly where you are meant to be and you're heading in the exact right direction!!</u>

Scientia potentia est. Knowledge is power and now you have all you need to put on your invisible Stress Ninja outfit and show life who's in charge! Print off the certificate on the next page and place it somewhere you can see it every day. Let it be a reminder that you are amazing and that this book is always there if you need help! X